MICRO ACTIVISM

How You Can
Make A Difference in the World
(Without A Bullhorn)

SMALL
ACTIONS
=
BIG
RESULTS

OMKARI L. WILLIAMS

foreword by Layla F. Saad

illustrations by Octavia Mingerink

Storey Publishing

T0036416

EDITED BY Liz Bevilacqua
ART DIRECTION AND BOOK DESIGN BY Carolyn Eckert
TEXT PRODUCTION BY Jennifer Jepson Smith
ILLUSTRATIONS BY © Octavia Ink of Pretty In Ink Press

Storey books are available at special discounts when purchased in bulk for premiums and sales promotions as well as for fund-raising or educational use. Special editions or book excerpts can also be created to specification. For details, please send an email to special.markets@hbgusa.com.

Storey Publishing
210 MASS MoCA Way
North Adams, MA 01247
storey.com

Storey Publishing, LLC is an imprint of Workman Publishing Co., Inc., a subsidiary of Hachette Book Group, Inc., 1290 Avenue of the Americas, New York, NY 10104

Distributed in Europe by Hachette Livre, 58 rue Jean Bleuzen, 92 178 Vanves Cedex, France
Distributed in the United Kingdom by Hachette Book Group, UK, Carmelite House, 50 Victoria Embankment, London EC4Y 0DZ

ISBNs: 978-1-63586-688-9 (paperback); 978-1-63586-689-6 (ebook)

Printed in the United States by Sheridan Books, Ltd.
10 9 8 7 6 5 4 3 2 1

Library of Congress Cataloging-in-Publication Data on file

MICRO
ACTIVISM

INTEGRITY

COMPASSION

CONVERSATION

COMMUNITY

HUMANITY

To the ancestors:
my grandparents,
Amos and Georgianna Williams
and Lionel and Miriam Guy,
and my glass-ceiling-shattering parents,
Vilma and Roy.

And to the future:
my nephews Elio and Miles,
because you deserve a beautiful world.

"Add your light to the sum of light."

LEO TOLSTOY

CONTENTS

For our activism
to be consistent,
it must also be
sustainable.
As in, for a lifetime,
not just a season.

Foreword by Layla F. Saad

I've always shied away from the title *activist*. Whenever I've been introduced as a guest on a podcast or as a speaker at a conference or even just to someone I'm meeting for the first time, I've always winced a bit when referred to as an activist.

Despite being an antiracism author and educator whose work is shared widely in activist and social justice spaces, I've always believed that activist is a title saved for a very specific type of person. When I pictured an archetypal activist in my mind, I saw someone leading protests in the streets or doing political organizing work or hosting fundraising events. But I hadn't pictured me: an author and speaker who writes and teaches largely from the comfort of her own home. I have a global platform but I'm not doing as much on-the-ground work. My work may agitate or activate people, but still affords me relative safety.

So, when someone calls me an activist I demure. I worry that I could be minimizing the work I know so many people are doing behind the scenes and on the front lines. At the same time, I know that many people see public figures like myself as activists precisely because our work reaches so many people. An archetypal activist in their minds may be a best-selling author or the founder of a justice movement or simply someone who has a lot of followers on social media.

The truth is, while we're fretting over who is or is not worthy of being called an activist, we are forgetting that activism is a *verb*, not a noun. It is a *practice*, not a title. As Omkari Williams brilliantly lays out in this book, activism is about doing the deep and devoted work of lifelong change-making. Activism means taking consistent action on the social causes that are most important to you.

For our activism to be consistent, it must also be sustainable. As in, for a lifetime, not just a season. And for it to be sustainable it has to make sense in the context of who we are, what our lives look like, what we're skilled at, what inspires us, and what our capacity is. It all starts with us—that is one of the first things I learned from Omkari Williams.

I first met Omkari in an online course. As the only Black women in the class, we immediately gravitated to each other. Omkari reached out to me and asked if I wanted to have a video call. We became fast friends and felt as though we'd known each other all our lives. Later that year we had the joy of meeting in person at a leadership conference in Georgia. During that conference, Omkari led a session on the importance of owning our personal stories and using them to create change in the world in our own unique way. I found this so powerful.

Too often we are encouraged to look at everyone else, measure and compare ourselves, and then try to force ourselves into ways of being that just don't fit. Unfortunately, we carry this into our activism and change-making work, believing that there is one right way or one desirable way to change the world. This reflects the very paradigms of hierarchy, supremacy, and dominance that we need to dismantle. And that's what micro activism is all about.

Micro activism helps us stop playing into the oppressive conditioning that teaches us to compete and compare. Instead, it teaches us that exactly who we are and what we bring to the table is precisely the kind of activism the world needs. There is space and necessity for all the activist types mentioned in this book: the Indispensables, Producers, Organizers, and Headliners. Being one or another isn't more right or more important. All are needed.

Each of us, consistently committed to our own practice of micro activism and working together as a collective, is what will actually create the healing and liberation we all desire. We don't need everyone founding movements or everyone being community organizers or everyone running social

Micro activism . . . teaches us that exactly who we are and what we bring to the table is precisely the kind of activism the world needs.

impact businesses or everyone hosting book clubs and podcasts. We don't all need to start a revolution. But we do need to figure out the part we are here to play in fighting racism, sexism, and all other -*isms* that deny human beings their humanity and harm the earth.

If, like me, you shy away from the title of activist or don't know if what you have to offer is enough or even important, this book will show you otherwise. You will walk away knowing that your unique way of being a changemaker is valid and valuable. And you will have the tools and mindset to ensure that you're joyfully in this work for the long haul. Because your activism will not just be what you do. It will reflect who you are.

WELCOME
I'M *SO* GLAD YOU PICKED UP THIS BOOK!

I'm guessing you did so because you're looking for a way of making a difference that fits in your life. A way of making a difference that doesn't ask you to make activism your career. You are in the right place.

You Don't Need a Bullhorn

Maybe you hear the word *activist* and think: That's great, but that's not me. Maybe it's because the word is too often defined in narrow terms, as something that requires giving speeches, leading marches, or taking other types of bold public action. But what if you actually can make a difference without standing on a stage or using a bullhorn? In fact, you can.

What if there is a way for you to make an impact on the social justice causes that you most care about without being an "influencer"?

What matters is that you are regularly taking action to make a difference. In fact, I believe that for most people, the most sustainable form of activism is micro activism.

- →

What if there is a way for you to do the work that calls to your heart without giving up the rest of your life and responsibilities?

What if all the small, sustained actions that unknown millions of people do are actually what moves the needle on prison reform, reproductive rights, LGBTQIA+ rights, housing for all, racial equity, solutions to the climate crisis, and all the other causes that people are working on every day?

What if there are as many ways of being an activist as there are people on the planet? What if an activist looks like . . . you?

Activism Means Taking Consistent Action

Being an activist means that you are someone who takes consistent action, whether you are front and center or behind the scenes, to advance a cause that you are passionate about. That's my definition of activism. For me, the size of the action isn't the point, nor is how vigorous the action is. What matters is that you are regularly taking action to make a difference. In fact, I believe that for most people, the most sustainable form of activism is micro activism.

When you think about the world, maybe you see all the things that are wrong, and all the broken places. You want to

↓

↓

↓

do something to make a difference, but you feel overwhelmed by the enormity of the challenges. Or maybe you know exactly where you want to put your efforts, and you know that the path of activism isn't one we walk alone; you're looking for some guidance to help you add your talents to the larger mix. Perhaps you are somewhere in between.

No matter where you find yourself on your activist journey, this book will help guide you. It will pose questions to help you discover your way of making a contribution and having a positive impact on the things you care about.

There is a lot going on in the world: a lot to deal with, a lot to think about, a lot of difference to be made. But none of us can do it all. None of us is meant to do it all. Finding a way to choose which causes to put your efforts toward—from all the ones that call to you—will help you make the impact you would like to make.

This is where life meets activism and activism meets life.

What I Know for Sure

The following six principles help me stay on the path when I am feeling pulled in a thousand directions, when I'm discouraged by how much there is to do, or when I witness harm. They keep me focused on what truly matters. If you share some or all of my guiding principles, we can create some activist magic here.

6-PRINCIPLE MANIFESTO

1. INTEGRITY IS KEY.

When we are being true to ourselves and our principles, we find stillness amid the storm. From that point of stillness, we can more readily take in stride the setbacks we encounter along the way to our goal.

2. JUSTICE EQUALS FREEDOM.

True justice lets us put down the burdens of anger and revenge. Where there is true justice, there is freedom for all of us.

3. STORIES MATTER.

Stories connect us to one another and reveal our shared humanity where we might otherwise miss it.

4. COMPASSION IS REQUIRED.

Without compassion for self, there is no compassion for others. Without compassion for others, there is no compassion for self.

5. JOY HELPS.

Joy helps us through the hard times. Joy points us to what's possible even amid struggle.

6. LOVE WINS.

Love is always the right choice.

You Can't (and Shouldn't) Take It All On

The world we are living in is facing unprecedented crises—from climate change to racism to the inequities highlighted by a global pandemic to the rise of authoritarianism. Each of these crises is significant but put them together and we are challenged to step up as never before. It can feel like the world is on the brink of collapse. If we were to try to take on all the challenges, we would be overwhelmed.

But taking it all on has never been possible and certainly is not what this moment calls for. What is needed instead is for each of us to take on the one thing that speaks most strongly to us, whether that's animal rights, reproductive rights, anti-racism work, climate change, food security, healthcare equity, voting rights, or something else altogether. We are not able (or meant) to fix everything; we're meant to work to fix what we can. That's the power of engaging in and nurturing micro activism.

Throughout this book, you will meet ordinary people who are making a difference with their activism. Most of them are micro activists; their activism is one part of their very full lives, not their main work. Others started as micro activists and then their activist passion became their main work. The point is that activists span the spectrum, and all contributions are needed. That includes yours.

While some activists are on a national or even an international stage, most of us can make an impact in our own backyards. That means doing our activist work on a small scale, working in collaboration with our local communities, our neighbors, or maybe even just one other person.

What Micro Activism Looks Like

Micro activism might be creating a community garden that brings fresh fruit and vegetables to those living in a food desert. It might be working with a literacy program at the local high school. It could be bringing visual or performing arts to kids who are not typically exposed to art. Or it might be knocking on doors to encourage people to exercise their right to vote.

Your small actions build one on the other and, collectively, have more of an impact than you might realize. Everyone has one gift or another that can be of use in service to a local community and, by extension, the global community. The key is to uncover your unique gift and then use it alongside other people to make the difference that only you can make.

Yes, it would be wonderful to end world hunger, but if you feed one person, doesn't that matter? It certainly matters to the person you feed.

One of the places that we get stuck in the conversation around activism is in thinking that activists are a select group of people, those comfortable with being in the spotlight and on the national or world stage. While that is certainly a section of activists, most do their work quietly, often way out of the view of those not in their communities. Some of those quiet workers are profiled in this book. Each is an activist in their own way. Each is making a difference in their community, and all their actions matter. Activism isn't just for those in the spotlight; it's also for those who want to help make things better right where they are planted. You have the power to make a positive difference; let's find your way and get on with the business of making the world a better place for us and for generations to come.

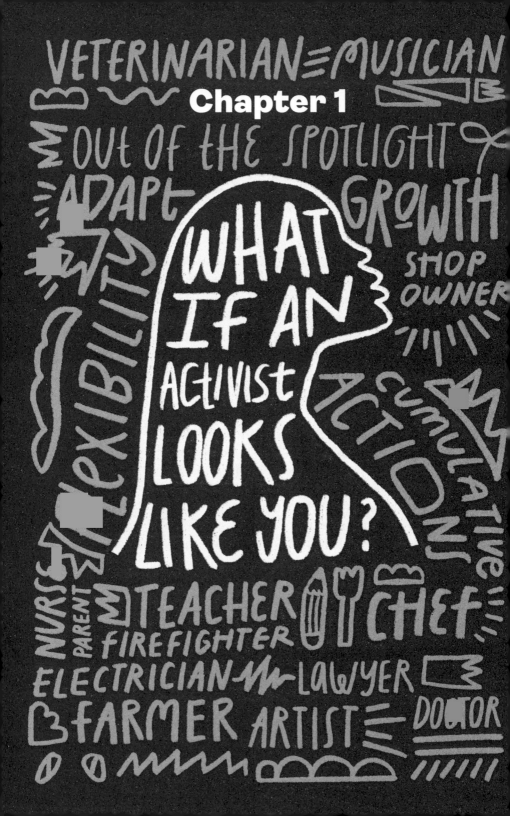

➡ The Heart of Activism

Activist. Whose faces pop into your head when you hear or see that word? Dr. Martin Luther King Jr., Nelson Mandela, Greta Thunberg, Malala Yousafzai, Rosa Parks, Gandhi, Desmond Tutu, Cesar Chavez, the Dalai Lama? Each person on that list is absolutely an activist, no argument. But these folks are just a tiny part of a much larger whole that includes millions of people around the world doing their part without acclaim or attention.

Those out-of-the-spotlight people are the heart of activism. And I'm going to guess there is a face you didn't see when you read the word *activist* above: yours.

When we think about activists, we typically think about people who are the face of a movement. We don't think about all the people working behind the scenes. But if the only people who qualified as activists were those bold faces and names familiar to us, nothing would get done. We would be no further along in the fight for racial justice, gender justice, and climate justice, to name just a few of the causes people around the world are working on every minute of every day. We would be no further along because significant change doesn't happen without the efforts of many, many people, the overwhelming majority of whom we will never know: deeply committed, often quiet, everyday activists making their small yet essential contributions to the collective, without fanfare.

Big Isn't for Everyone

We live in a world that celebrates the big, the bold, the noteworthy. We live in a world that tends to diminish the small actions with statements like "Go big or go home." But big isn't for everyone, big isn't what is needed in every case, and while big can be great, so can small. The small, cumulative actions are the ones that add up to the big change. The small, often unnoticed actions are the ones that create the tipping point.

In 1955, nine months before a Black seamstress named Rosa Parks refused to give up her seat to a white passenger on a bus in Montgomery, Alabama, a 15-year-old girl named Claudette Colvin was arrested in the same city for doing the same thing. Then, two months before Parks's arrest, an 18-year-old girl named Mary Louise Smith was arrested for refusing to yield her seat. Few people know the names and stories of the teenagers, whose actions were spontaneous, but resistance to racial segregation had long been planned. Did you know that Rosa Parks had received extensive training to prepare her to resist Jim Crow laws? Civil rights leaders

If the only people who qualified as activists were those in the spotlight, nothing would get done.

- →

selected her to be the face of that fight because she was better positioned to withstand the rigors of it, including death threats, than the two younger women were.

Although inspired by Parks's activism, the Montgomery bus boycott succeeded because of all the unknown Black people who, for 13 long months, did not take the bus. It ended only when the U.S. Supreme Court upheld a ruling that deemed bus segregation unconstitutional.

I love this example of the Montgomery bus boycott because it shows how critical community participation is. It was the steadfast refusal of Black residents to take the bus—no matter how hot, wet, or cold it was—that forced the change. Many showed creativity in organizing carpools and in driving cabs that charged the same fare as the buses. Others walked miles, adding hours onto their workdays. Who were those people? I don't know their names, but I know that, without them and their dedication to the cause of justice, Jim Crow laws would have continued far longer than they did.

Don't Underestimate the Power of Unglamorous Tasks

I like glamour as much as the next person. The charismatic speaker, the grand gesture—these are compelling, no question. But they're also the outliers. All the while, behind the scenes,

It is the critical mass of people standing up for what they believe in that ultimately moves the needle toward justice.

---→

other people are doing work that makes the great speech or the grand gesture possible.

When we're watching a movie, we see the actors in all their glory. What we don't see are the film crew, the wardrobe team, the hair and makeup people, and the craft services employees who kept everyone fed during the filming. We don't notice the names that scroll by in the closing credits; we just see the main show. But without all those other people, the film wouldn't even exist.

It's the same with activism: While the people who are the face of a movement have a crucial role to play, so does everyone else. It is the critical mass of people standing up for what they believe in that ultimately moves the needle toward justice. Take the unsung heroes out of the picture, and nothing changes.

Discover Your Personal Activist Style

Each of us has our unique way of doing activist work. It's a mix of our personality traits and how those interact with the activist cause and the circumstances surrounding us.

You've likely experienced a circumstance that forced you outside your normal comfort zone of response. Maybe you typically avoid confrontation, but if someone verbally attacks your child, you might speak up without hesitation. Or maybe you have no problem using your voice, but you hold your tongue to let your child stand up and learn how to advocate for herself.

What is happening around us impacts how we respond to a circumstance; none of us is the same person in every situation. For example, millions of people around the world who had never been to a march in their lives took to the streets in the wake of George Floyd's murder by a Minneapolis police officer in May 2020. Their grief and outrage propelled them into an action that had previously been foreign to them. The moment in which you find yourself matters. Allow yourself to embrace the flexibility that comes with responding to that moment.

The Four Activist Archetypes

I've identified four overarching types of activists. Nobody is 100 percent one type, but most of us have a type or two that predominate. The archetypes can give us valuable information about our most comfortable, and therefore most sustainable, way of doing activist work. Identifying your type will help you craft a plan of activism that you can maintain and grow with over time.

Take the Activist Archetype Quiz

Go to page 155 and take the Activist Archetype Quiz to find out what kind of activist you are. Then come back here and learn more about your archetype. You can also take the quiz online at omkariwilliams.com /activist-archetype-quiz.

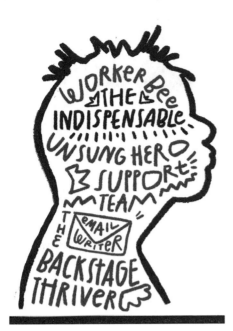

THE INDISPENSABLE: You are one of the many people working in the background to make change.

THE PRODUCER: You create the schedule and make sure that nothing falls through the cracks.

THE ORGANIZER: You keep things on schedule and address the various assignments.

THE HEADLINER: You are the face of the movement, the person who inspires those who seek the same change you do.

→ THE INDISPENSABLE

You want to conduct your activism as far out of the spotlight as possible. Being center stage is your idea of torture. So you are backstage, doing the unsung work that keeps things moving. Thankfully, you are among millions of other people who are happy to do such work. Fortunately, you recognize that the value of the work you do doesn't correlate to how well known you are. It suits you just fine to keep the office running while others take the public-facing roles.

Or maybe you are out marching with your family and friends and dozens (or millions) of others for a shared cause. Or perhaps marching isn't your thing, and you prefer instead to make sure the marchers in your life have water, snacks, sunscreen, and anything else they might need.

To support an organization, you could be answering phones, stuffing envelopes, making coffee, or creating posters—making your voice heard by bolstering the people who are committed to your cause so that those with the power to make a difference, those with the power to change policies, can't ignore you.

Your specialty might be writing letters to the editor or emails to your elected officials. Expressions of opinion can move the needle, and you don't even have to get out of your pajamas to write them.

You shun the spotlight, but that doesn't mean you aren't dedicated to change. Don't underestimate your importance. Without you, and millions like you, nothing happens.

Indispensables include every person at a march for social justice causes, as well as all those people in the trenches doing the unglamorous work every day—those whose names we will never hear but without whom the change we seek would never occur.

The Producer

You are happiest when engaged in small groups. You love supporting the more outgoing members of your community and want little attention on yourself. Your emphasis is on maintaining the big picture so that others can play their essential roles in your common effort. You are great at seeing how the parts fit together and making sure that nothing gets missed. At the end of the day, the thing you want most is to accomplish your community's larger goal. You'll be just offstage, cheering loudly, when that goal is achieved.

When a march is announced, you spring into action. You break down the elements of the event: Where and when will it occur? What permits will you need? Are there any security concerns? You organize a medical team in case of emergency, figure out where marchers can find restrooms and water, gather information on what to do if there are counterprotesters, and take care of dozens of other details. Once you've made your list, you start delegating tasks. Then you stay on top of things to make sure nothing falls through the cracks. It's likely that no one outside your organization knows who you are— and that's exactly how you like it.

Examples of Producers include campaign managers and social media directors.

THE ORGANIZER

You have mad organizational skills, and your idea of a good time is putting those skills to work for a cause that matters to you. You can implement the various aspects of a plan and bring your administrative expertise to bear.

You are the person who prefers to stay behind the scenes but will step into the spotlight if need be. Your superpower is creating detailed action steps to move your group toward its overarching goal.

You are happy giving the Headliner (described below) the support they need. You know how valuable your ability to step into the spotlight is when the Headliner needs a break. Then you are more than happy to go back to working behind the scenes.

Your two specialties are keeping things on track for the Headliner and translating the Producer's plan into actionable steps that your community can implement. You are fond of spreadsheets and lists of all sorts. You are serious about your responsibility to execute the task you're given. Without you, things would get messy really quickly.

Organizers include Rosa Parks (also a Headliner), the late U.S. representative Elijah Cummings (who spent his 23 years in Congress working to pass legislation to help poor and working-class Americans), and that person in your local arts organization who creates the brilliant spreadsheet to keep everything and everyone on track for the goal of getting funding from your city council.

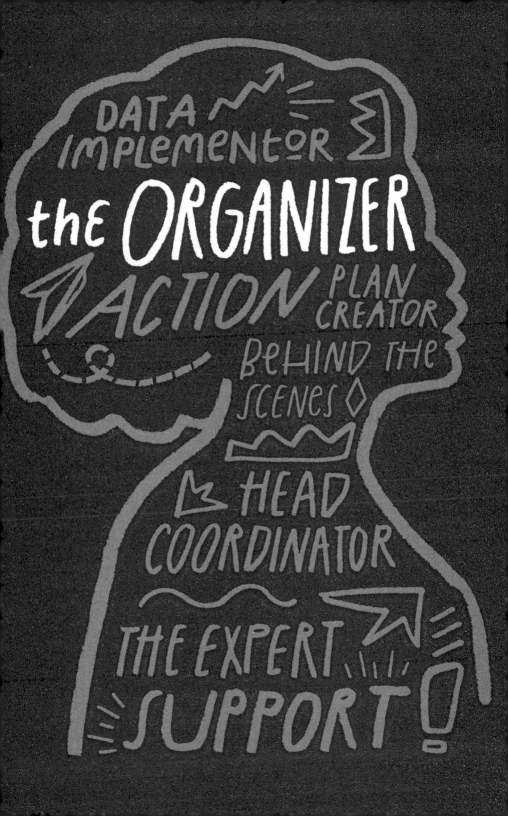

THE HEADLINER

You are in your element in a leadership position. Taking action is what you do. Standing up and speaking to 10 people or 10,000 feels the same to you. You are comfortable in the spotlight, and you know that this gives you the opportunity to powerfully connect with large numbers of people.

You have a big vision, and it's second nature for you to go out and talk about that vision. Bringing people into your cause is satisfying—not for the attention you get, but for the impact you can make. You are an expert in your area of activism, and you make sure that you keep learning because you have a responsibility to those who look to you for leadership.

You hold the larger vision of what is possible so that you can help plan and implement strategies that will move your group toward its goal. You look for the intersections between your cause and those of others in order to build your constituency and, as a result, your organization's power.

You know that the point of power is not for your personal use or ego; power means more ears listening to what you have to say, more eyes on your cause, and more decision-makers recognizing that they have to take you seriously.

You understand the burden that comes with being the face of a cause, and you accept that burden because what you are fighting for is so important to you. You know there likely will be slings and arrows coming your way, but they will not deter you. You have a job to do, a cause to fight for, and people to inspire and lead.

Headliners include Greta Thunberg, Martin Luther King Jr., Gloria Steinem, Angela Davis, and Malala Yousafzai.

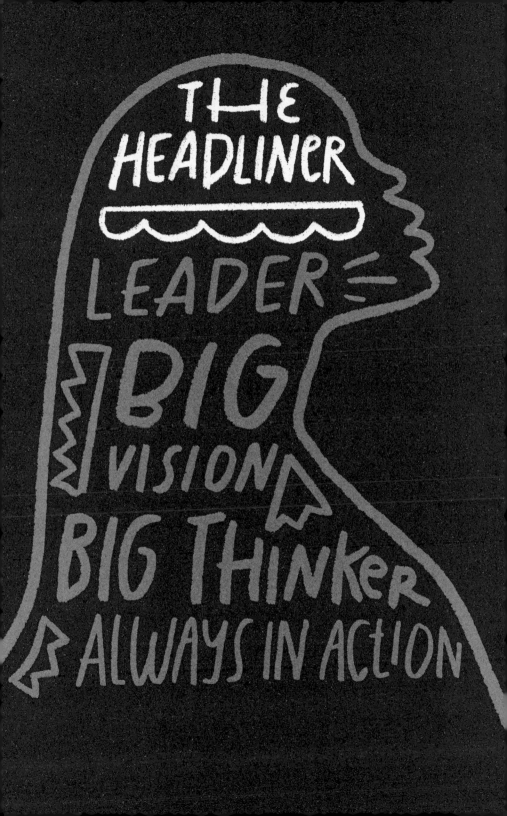

Stay Flexible in Your Archetype

One of the lovely things about being human is that growth and change are always available to us. We learn new things, and that new knowledge changes how we act. We meet new people, and they inspire us to think about things differently, to try new things, and to be braver than we might have believed ourselves to be. We aren't static, and neither are the causes we are fighting for.

Allowing yourself to grow and change in your activism is part of the process. Sometimes growth is fast and furious; at other times growth means quietly doing research and expanding your base of knowledge. At still other times, growth means building community and finding where you fit in to that community at this particular point in your life.

Don't feel that you must stick strictly to your archetype. The causes you are advocating for are ever evolving. There are triumphs and setbacks, and you will have to adapt to the changing landscape. Recognize that while you have your essential archetype, you will also have elements of other archetypes depending on what is needed. Flexibility is critical in crafting a plan of activism that suits you, an activism that you can grow with, and a plan of action you can sustain over the long term. Sometimes events will force you into actions much bolder or much smaller than the ones you might normally take. Yes, you have your dominant archetype, but that is not the whole of who you are and what you're capable of. Keeping your ultimate goal in mind and being responsive, not reactive, is what you're aiming for.

Your Activist Type Is a Guide

Use your archetype as a guide to find the ways that make the most sense for you to engage in your activism, not as a way of limiting your creativity. We are all multifaceted, and that applies to our activism as much as any other area of our life. Think about some activists who inspire you (don't forget people in your community). Take a moment: How does it feel to realize that an activist looks like you?

Remember, most of us are not Headliners. Most activists work out of the spotlight. Here are a few ways to participate in activism that don't require a stage or a bullhorn.

Activist Work Outside the Spotlight

▶ Designing websites or graphics, and/or providing tech support

▶ Writing policy proposals, letters to the editor, or emails to elected officials

▶ Provoking new ways of thinking by telling stories, creating visual art, staging theatrical productions, writing songs or poems, or making crafts

▶ Sharing resources, weaving connections, and supporting other activists to strengthen and sustain movements while ensuring community care

▶ Organizing support for a Headliner event, such as making sure there are flyers to hand out, T-shirts to give away, water to drink, and bathrooms to access

▶ Researching what legal support is available (as when Muslims were banned from entering the United States in early 2017 and immigration lawyers were needed for people trapped at points of entry)

▶ Feeding the people who are out doing the more public-facing work

▶ "Calling in" friends on social media (that is, recognizing a problem and using kindness rather than shame to invite them to act on the issue) and having difficult conversations with loved ones (a skill we all can use)

▶ Having a bake sale at your kids' school for a cause

▶ Getting your kids involved so that they grow up understanding that they have the power to make a difference

Lure Wishes

Blue Mountains National Park, Australia

What goal are you working toward?

Care for the earth, oceans, forests, rivers, and sky; and a kind, loving, and just relationship with Indigenous people.

What motivates you?

Nature has always been my haven and home. I was born in a small town in New South Wales, Australia, and I've always been most at home in wild places. It's broken my heart to witness the destruction of the wild and ancient forests. The town of my birth had a relatively large Aboriginal population. I remember being confused as a child, as I looked around, not understanding the divisions within the town, the separation, racism, and injustice. This sent me on a mission to learn more. I learned about the history of this country. I started visiting remote areas of the country, tutoring Aboriginal teenagers at a boarding school in Central Australia in the evenings, and working with Aboriginal artists during the day. I went on to live and work with Aboriginal adults in the remote far northwest of the country. Throughout this, my questions remained, and disturbance grew. I turned more and more towards wanting to understand what it is within us that enables and perpetuates these circumstances, and to how we might unravel it all and find another way.

How do you find and build community?

My sense of community has expanded and now includes the greater sphere of relationships with the land, trees, ocean, rivers, and the rest of life. I connect there, and this sustains me through

> My sense of community has expanded and now includes the greater sphere of relationships with the land, trees, ocean, rivers, and the rest of life.

all the challenges we all live through. I live in a small village in the Blue Mountains National Park. I met a wonderful group of local activists during a stay here a few years ago, and I recently joined up with a local group working towards reconciliation and relationship with Aboriginal people locally. Beyond that, there's all the loving connections with kindred spirits across the world, met through various groups, events, and experiences, in person and online. I treasure them.

Who are your role models?

My grandmother Jessie Hayes, and how I felt while she sat knitting silently while fiery debates raged around her among other family members. I remember one afternoon, looking over at her, feeling like she was knitting the world back together.

What keeps you going when things are hard?

The land, the oceans, the forests, and this beautiful earth. More and more my sense of the treasure and finiteness of this life of mine. There's so much I want to share and can feel the limits of this window I have to do so. My friends. Poetry. Music. Beauty. My ancestors with their guidance, support, and healing. They help me remember my place in this world, and call me sometimes to do more, sometimes to rest more, and always love.

Do you have an intentional practice of self-care?

Sitting silently in nature, singing to the trees and the waterways. Listening, mostly.

Reflect on Your Activist Type

▶ **What kind of activist tasks** am I comfortable doing? Try to come up with at least 10. Don't judge them by their size or impact.

▶ **What are some tasks** outside my comfort zone that I might take on? Try to come up with at least three.

▶ **What are some skills** so natural to me that I tend to dismiss their potential usefulness, for example, letter writing, bookkeeping, or visual art?

Chapter Takeaways

There is **NO ONE WAY** of being an
activist. Each of us has our own way.

We're a **COMBINATION** of activist types,
and the circumstances we find
ourselves in will determine how we
show up as activists.

Use your type as a guide
for ways in which you can make your
CONTRIBUTION.

↓
↓
↓

Chapter 2

LAY YOUR FOUNDATION

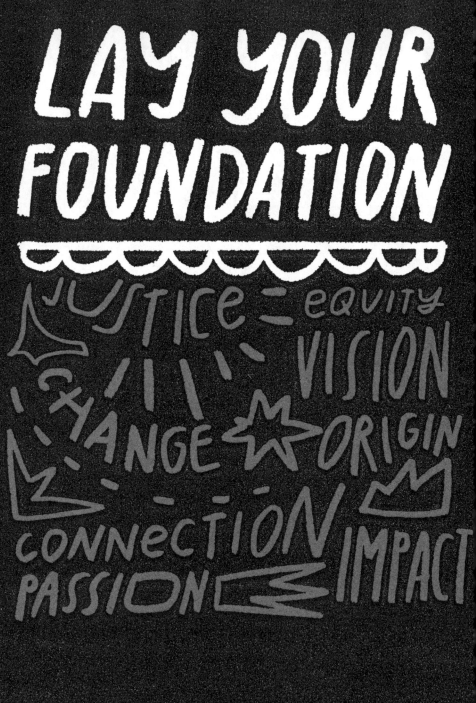

→ The Power of Story

The starting point for all activism is becoming aware of something that strikes you as wrong or unjust and deciding that you want to make a difference. You don't yet have to know how to change the thing that you want to change; you just have to know that you want things to be different. You have a vision that there is a better way of doing things, a different idea of how the world should look, or a different way we should be treating others. But before you can seek change, you need to identify what, specifically, you are trying to achieve. A teacher of mine once said that we can't find our way home if we don't know that's where we're going. That has stuck with me over the years. So where are you going? What is the story you want to change or create?

Those arguing for environmental sustainability are trying to write a new story about how we care for this fragile planet. Those fighting for the rights of LGBTQIA+ people are working to write a new story about who we are as humans beyond concepts of gender and sexuality. Those working for reproductive rights are trying to write a new story about bodily autonomy that isn't based on outdated ideas of women as the property of men. (Did you know that in the United States a woman could not get a credit card without a man's signature until 1974?!) All these examples come down to the stories that we tell, individually and collectively. These stories then determine how we behave and what laws get passed.

Discover Your Origin Story

It's likely that you have a personal story related to the thing you want to change. This is your origin story. An origin story typically arises from an event that occurred that propelled you from observer to participant. Origin stories often come from lived experience. Maybe you were bullied as a child or witnessed someone being bullied, and ever since then bullying is something that has bothered you deeply. Your step into activism was when you learned about the link between bullying and school shootings and decided to do what you can in your local school to address this problem.

My story has roots in the work that my father did in the world. Dad was a humanitarian who spent time in places like Bosnia during the war there and Rwanda during the genocide. He didn't speak to me much about what he witnessed, but I saw his unshakable commitment to easing the path for those who were victims of disasters, both natural and manmade: those whose suffering too often goes unseen, whose voices too often go unheard. I know that his inability to fix all that was wrong weighed heavily on him even though he knew,

The story of the event that propelled you into action is, at least in part, your origin story.

--→

intellectually, he couldn't possibly fix everything. Watching Dad struggle with that reality contributed to my ideas about radical realism. (I will talk more about radical realism in Chapter 3.) I know myself well enough to know that I need to be realistic in order to stay in the work. I don't know what Dad's origin story was—I'm not even sure he thought about things that way—but his work is part of mine.

The story of the event that propelled you into action is, at least in part, your origin story. At this stage, you don't need to know what you're going to do with your origin story. You just need to start thinking about how it has impacted you and begin to consider what work it might lead you to. Or if you're already in action, you can think about how consciously connecting to that story might inform your work going forward.

Connect to Your Origin Story

Stories impact us in many ways; sometimes we don't even understand why a particular story hits us so powerfully. Once you have discovered your story, you must then connect to it, because when the going gets hard (which it will in activism, as in the rest of life), that connection will help keep you from stopping when you're discouraged and quitting seems like an option.

Connecting to our story not only helps us maintain our motivation but also helps us understand others and their

↓
↓
↓

motivations. Story is a deep part of our human experience. When we meet someone and start to spend time with them, what we share is our stories. We use our stories to reveal who we are and what we care about. We use stories to connect with those who share our concerns and passions, and those shared stories lead us to finding and building our communities.

Our shared understanding of experiences is the foundation of our friendships and intimate relationships. When we connect with someone, it's because we share a way of looking at the world. We share an interpretation of things that have happened, both to us personally and in the larger world. It is our shared stories, our shared experiences that build the bonds of relationships, including our relationships with those who share an activist passion with us.

As you start to build your micro activism practice, be sure that you are solidly connected to the stories that live at the heart of what you care about and the change you want to help bring forth in the world.

Foster Collective Belonging

As a little Black girl growing up with well-educated parents in a middle-class home in Manhattan, I felt like there was nowhere I truly belonged. My skin color kept me apart from the white kids I knew; we were friendly, but there was always the awareness that I was different. My family's economic and educational status isolated me from some of the other Black kids I knew whose families were less well-off than mine. Being told that I sounded white by one group and being asked where I learned to speak so well by the other made clear to me that I did not belong in either of the worlds I was moving in.

In the widest perspective, activism and social justice involve creating a world where everyone belongs. Black, Brown, female, gender-fluid, queer, and poor folks—as well as many other currently marginalized groups—should be included in the sphere of power and importance.

A sense of belonging is a basic human desire, and expanding it for ourselves and others is at the heart of the work we are doing. If you base your work on the foundation of recognizing that, truly, we all belong, you will ask questions like these: Who currently feels welcome here, and who does not? What are the obstacles that have been put up to collective belonging? Whom do those obstacles serve? Whom do they harm? How do we redress the balance so that belonging becomes the norm in our organization? How do we work, both as individuals and as groups, to achieve that goal?

Keeping the value of collective belonging at the forefront of your activist work will help you avoid falling into the trap of isolating yourself from other people doing work across other areas of activism. If you hold collective belonging as the goal to which we all aspire, then you can take a more charitable approach when someone does something that feels harmful or wrong. We all want to belong. That is what we, with our inevitable stumbles and missteps, are working toward.

REMOVING BARRIERS AND RESTRICTIONS IN ACTIVISM

The goal of collective belonging removes barriers and allows all of us to find our place in the world determined by our interests and qualities of character rather than our externally assigned identities of race or class or gender or socioeconomic status. These labels are a way of keeping people in separate silos rather than connecting as members of the human family and engaging in respectful communion with the natural world.

Imagine for a moment what it would feel like not to be restricted by your identity and to simply be you, following the interests that you have and living a life not circumscribed by being labeled as this or that. If you have a hard time imagining this, I completely understand. It is far from where we are now, but that is truly the goal. To be, as Dr. Martin Luther King Jr. said, judged by the content of our character, not the color of our skin, or any other label of identity.

WHAT DOES INCLUSION REALLY MEAN?

The word *inclusion* has been used a lot lately. I actually don't like this word, because *including* someone means that someone else still has ownership over membership decisions. If, instead, we believe that we all belong, simply by virtue of existing, then we understand that we can't give belonging to, or take it from, someone. Belonging is simply part of what comes with being here on earth. If we all belong, then there is respect for the part that each of us plays in this life. And along with respect come care and dignity and openness to the opinions of others, particularly those most impacted by the issue we are working on. No matter the subject, listening to those people who are most impacted by the issue will offer a path of respect, understanding, and, ultimately, belonging.

RACIAL EQUITY LIES AT THE ROOT OF ALL ACTIVIST WORK

Racial justice touches every kind of activism, from climate change to reproductive rights to food security and beyond. The social construct of race has historically determined where people with power focus their time, attention, money, and resources. Climate change, for example, most dramatically impacts communities of color. World leaders are dragging their feet as we hurtle toward becoming a planet that cannot support life. Understanding the role that race plays in the decisions that our leaders make is critical to shifting our world toward sustainability and justice. If the impacts of climate change were hitting predominantly white countries at the same rate they are hitting countries that are mostly Black and

Brown, perhaps global leaders would be treating this crisis with the urgency it demands.

As many scholars have pointed out, race is a social (not biological) construct created in the 1600s to justify and support the enslavement of Africans by arguing that they, by virtue of the color of their skin, were subhuman. That construct was extended to Indigenous people, Asian people, and even dark-skinned European people. When we look at race with this awareness, we begin to see how this false way of determining the value of certain people has permeated our society.

Racism and antiracism will come up in any activist cause you choose to work on. We cannot dismantle oppressive systems or exploitative structures without confronting racism. If race is the determinant for the value of people, then it's easy to justify stealing land, freedom, traditions, resources, and life itself from those deemed less valuable. If race is the determinant of somebody's value, it's easy to pollute areas that are home to people of color. It is easy to apply different rules to those deemed less valuable, and to systematically regulate, restrict, and punish them.

Dr. Ibram X. Kendi writes wonderfully about these issues in his book *How to Be an Antiracist*. For more information about antiracism work, I encourage you to explore the resources section at the back of this book (page 171). As you engage in this work, I encourage you to be both persistent and kind with yourself and others. This is the work of a lifetime. We didn't get here overnight, and we won't get out of here overnight. But the rewards outweigh the challenges—just keep going.

Waylon "Pee" Pahona

Navajo Nation

What are you working toward?

I have created a sustainable space on social media for Indigenous people to share wellness stories and to share the struggles they have been through on the journey. We started with 100 people, and now we are up to 75,000 members.

What motivates you?

I've never really seen myself as an activist, but as a protector of my people. I was sexually abused as a child, and I've seen a lot of things a child should not experience. It led me to attempt to take my life in 2007. That completely changed me, and I ended up getting help and I became a personal trainer. I used myself and my story to help others get healthy through positive mindset.

What does your work look like?

I work as a personal trainer, and I am currently working in outpatient recovery centers helping my Indigenous brothers and sisters.

How do you find and build community?

I have traveled across the United States and Canada sharing my story and helping others heal.

Who are your role models?

Vernon Masayesva is one of my role models. He has been fighting for water rights for Indigenous people for many years, and he has motivated me to push forward.

> I've never really seen myself
> as an activist, but as a protector
> of my people.

What keeps you going?

Knowing that I've made it through sexual abuse, through seeing my father accidentally kill a 3-year-old child, through having to revive my mother as a teen when she tried to take her life. All these things that I have endured as a young child molded me into the man I am today.

What would you tell your activist self from 10 years ago?

I would tell myself to pay close attention to all the questions I have about my life. Eventually those answers will come; you just need to be patient.

What do you want to tell your future activist self?

Continue the journey and keep learning about yourself. You have a long way to go, but push forward.

Do you have an intentional practice of self-care?

I like to meditate and walk early in the morning. One time I walked 200 miles in 8 days and learned so much about myself and grew from that experience.

Determine What You Stand For

Often in activist work, people come at the question of what they stand for from the opposite side; they talk about what they are against. While there is value in knowing what you're against, there is far more power in knowing what you are for.

Do a little experiment right now: Pause for a moment to settle yourself, take a deep inhale and a full exhale, and return to your normal breathing. Now think of something that you are against. Child abuse, for example. Say aloud: "I am against child abuse." Now try saying: "I am for all children living lives of security and joy." Which feels more motivating in your body?

What we stand against brings a burst of hot anger and passion. These are appropriate and necessary feelings, but they are hard to sustain and likely to lead to burnout. Expressing the desired change in terms of what we are for is far more grounding, sustainable, and empowering than a single-minded focus on what we are against. Both *against* and *for* are important, yet from the perspective of doing the work, what we are for is more useful to us over the long haul.

WRITE A
"WHAT I STAND FOR" LIST

- **Ask yourself, "What do I stand for?"**
  What springs to mind? Maybe you think of
  animal rights, homes for the unhoused, racial justice,
  reproductive rights, clean oceans, clean water,
  affordable healthcare for all, education that
  encourages children to think critically, or LGBTQIA+
  rights. I could go on, because there is no shortage
  of causes that need advocacy.

- **Do you feel overwhelmed by the question?**
  Do so many things need fixing that you can't figure
  out where to start, and so you default to doing
  nothing? You are not alone. The sheer scope of
  things that need to be put right would overwhelm
  anyone, especially if you can't decide where to
  focus your efforts.

- **Take some time to make a list** of the causes
  that you currently care about. List everything you
  can think of that you care about enough to have
  considered donating time, energy, or money to.
  Get them all out of your head and into writing.

- **You've got your (possibly massive) list.**
  Now what to do with it? It's time to refine
  your focus.

The Noah's Ark Rule: Pick Two

Are you familiar with the story in the Bible about Noah's ark?
God tells Noah to build an ark, collect two of each type of
animal, and put them on the ark to save them from the coming
flood. Well, we can apply this rule to activism. Putting
your focus on just one or two issues can help you persist in
your activist work.

What do you do when picking only two can feel like
abandoning the rest of the deserving causes that are out there?
There is an enormous amount of need in the world. Any one
of the causes that made your "what I stand for" list is urgent
enough to focus on for an entire lifetime. When the need is
so massive, how do you choose? The first step is to return
to your origin story, because that story is deeply part of who
you are as a person and, ultimately, as an activist.

HOW TO NARROW YOUR FOCUS

When you think about your origin stories, which causes come
up first? Which is top of mind when you think about activist
work? Is it climate change? Maybe racial justice is the cause
that you can talk about for hours. Or perhaps the need to
ensure reproductive rights gets you going every time. Whatever
cause is the one that comes up first is an excellent place to
start, because you have a strong connection with that cause.
This connection could also be a story about someone else that
deeply impacted you. Whatever the spark is, pay attention to it.

When I tell people to focus on one cause, or at most two,
I often get pushback. People tell me that they care about so
many things that deciding what to focus on feels wrong. What
about the rest of the things that need doing? Yes, there is an
enormous amount that needs doing. But, fortunately, there
are about 8 billion people on the planet, and between all of us,
we've got everything covered. I promise you, no matter how
specific your particular cause, there is someone else working
on it somewhere. And, thanks to the power of the internet,

it's possible to find those people no matter where you or they are in the world.

I say this because it's important to realize that there is no way any of us can take on all the issues that feel important to us. If we want to be effective in our activist work, we have to decide where to put our time and energy. We have to trust that others out there are working on the things we care about but don't have the capacity to address.

FOCUS CREATES THE GREATEST IMPACT

We make our greatest impact when we direct our full attention to one or, at most, two causes that are important to us. A maximum of only two.

Look at your "what I stand for" list. Take the first two causes and decide which is most important. Cross off the one that doesn't make the cut. Then look at the cause that's left and the next one on your list; decide which of those two is most important. Keep going until you are down to two. This way, you're never evaluating more than two causes at a time and you won't feel overwhelmed. Once you've got your last two, decide if you want to focus on both or if you feel your time would be better spent on one issue.

This doesn't mean that you are wedded to this one (or two) cause(s) for the rest of your life. Events happen that change our focus. For me, when the Trump administration started putting children in cages on the southern border of the United States, that took immediate precedence over one of my other causes. I put my focus on that until people with more expertise and resources were able to put in place systems to address the situation. At that point, I turned my attention back to my primary causes.

Jessica Hesse

Greenfield, Massachusetts

What goal are you working toward?
Prison abolition.

What motivates you?
My involvement in activism started when I graduated college and moved into an intentional living situation in Boston. I lived in community with queer, disabled, BIPOC, radical feminists, organizers, abolitionists, and leftists. So much of what I've learned about social justice, racial justice, restorative and transformative justice, and abolition came from those extremely dedicated and generous folks who took me under their wings.

What does your work toward that goal look like?
I believe that we live in a society that profits off harm. My end goal is to help create a world where people are connected, liberated, have more than just their basic living needs met, and where every person can thrive and live the life they want to. This world, to me, looks like one where the prison industrial complex no longer exists, so that is what I strive for!

How do you find and build community?
When I moved to western Massachusetts, I found Books Through Bars. Because it is a collective, everyone has an equal stake in the work we do, and everyone's voice matters. I really like how just by going to a volunteer day and packing books, you can connect with other like-minded folks. And you are also making a material difference in the life of someone who is incarcerated by sending them reading materials to stave off

> **My end goal is to help create a world where people are connected . . . and where every person can thrive and live the life they want to.**

boredom, to learn, to take their minds elsewhere for a while, to make a connection with someone who society has tried to force us to forget.

Who are your role models?
I love Angela Davis, Ruth Wilson Gilmore, and Emma Goldman.

What keeps you going?
I really love Mariame Kaba's quote, "Hope is a discipline." When things are difficult, like you're throwing specks of sand instead of giant wrenches in the mechanisms that perpetuate oppression and violence, I always think of this quote and remember that even if in my lifetime I never see the end of incarceration, it's important to celebrate the small victories and to keep striving for what so many radical activists have been putting their lives on the line for.

What do you want to tell your future activist self?
You need to keep working activism into your lifestyle, and not to give up the fight.

Do you have an intentional practice of self-care?
I love to lie in bed or sit on the porch with a good book and a cup of tea or listen to an audiobook and relax. Reading and spending intentional time alone to recharge are the best things I do for self-care.

↓
↓
↓

HOW TO MAXIMIZE YOUR IMPACT

As activists who care about multiple issues, we have to recognize our own limitations and have faith that putting our attention on one or two issues doesn't mean that we are abandoning our interest in others that are equally important. It means that we are deciding to maximize our impact. We do the most service when we dive deeply in to our chosen area of work.

- ▶ What are the one or two causes that rose to the top of your list? What is your origin story for that area, or those areas, of focus? Spend a little time writing about your choice and what it means to you.

- ▶ When you are feeling discouraged or uncertain about your impact, return to your origin story and reconnect with your motivation for making this specific change in the world.

Chapter Takeaways

Your origin story connects you to **THE WHY** of your activist work and will sustain you.

Racial justice and equity work are **FOUNDATIONAL.**

What you are for is more **MOTIVATING** than what you are against.

Follow the **NOAH'S ARK RULE** and pick, at most, two causes to focus on at any time.

→ "Go Big or Go Home" Is Bad Advice

One of the keys to being able to sustain our activist work is to be radically realistic about our capacity. We live in a society that celebrates multitasking and enormous actions: "Go big or go home," people say. But the truth is, this isn't how things get done. It may look like that because we're only seeing the result of what is often years of work behind the scenes: years of building relationships and plans that bring to fruition a shared vision. It took hundreds of years of work by abolitionists before slavery became illegal in the United States.

Radical realism means recognizing that we can't do everything all at once; some things are going to take a long time. It also means making plans that are about moving things forward and persisting in the face of obstacles. Our culture has elevated "being busy" to the point that free time becomes a source of shame. But taking a break and having gaps in your schedule is the path to long-term success. We need time to rest, and we need time to assess. Building this time into your plans is essential to thrive.

Radical realism applies both to activist groups and to the individuals who comprise those groups. Your food justice collective may have a vision for addressing hunger in your community, but it won't be able to implement that vision if the members of the collective are burned out.

What are the multiple small steps that a food justice collective can take to reach the goal of ending hunger in your community? And how do you keep moving forward on incremental change without getting discouraged by the seeming lack of measurable progress?

No matter the goal, there will be many, many steps between where you are and where you want to be. There will be significant obstacles to confront. Micro activism shows us that the way to meaningful change is to take small actions, consistently, in the direction of the change we are seeking. Micro activism works best when we hold the long (macro) view and the short (micro) view at the same time.

Celebrate Micro Milestones

Micro activism is, well, *micro*, and we want to identify and celebrate milestones along the way—places where we can take a pause, acknowledge all that we have done, and savor the moment. I like to think of it this way: When babies are learning to walk, they are celebrated for each wobbly effort. One single step is an accomplishment. When—not *if* but *when*—they fall, they are encouraged to try again, with no negative judgment.

Radical realism allows us to apply that same approach to what we are doing as activists. We know that we are going to fall, we know that the whole process is going to take time, and we just keep going. Our focus is on the goal, and we value each bit of progress.

Determine Your Goal

Ask yourself, "What change am I committed to?" The answer to this question is the starting point. This question will guide you in deciding what to take on and lead you to ways in which you can contribute.

If your activist work is on racial justice, for example, then that means that you are aware that we each have biases and are willing to listen if someone points out a bias that you may be unaware of. It means that you hold the goal of racial justice at the forefront of your decision-making, both at work and in your personal life, so that your decisions are in alignment with your stated values.

Determining what your goal is also makes it easier to keep your focus when things get hard. When you find yourself at odds with colleagues and collaborators about how to do something, remembering what you're working toward can take the sting out of a disagreement and get you all back on task.

Clarity about your goal also makes it much easier to say yes or no to offers and opportunities. If a proposed action or event is not aligned with your mission, then it's an easy no. And if it is, then you get to look at it through the lens of possibility. You may or may not say yes, but the decision will be far easier when you know exactly what you're after.

Be Realistic about Your Time

Another core question that radical realism asks of you is, "What does sustainable action look like for me at this point in time? How much time do I realistically have to spend on activist work each week?"

One of the ways you can trip yourself up is when you decide you are going to commit to an action without considering what kind of bandwidth you truly have. Where are you in life? What other commitments and responsibilities do you have to fulfill?

It can be challenging to be realistic. Something happens—a legal ruling, a mass shooting, or an environmental disaster—and you get very energized to do something. I know that feeling of being pulled to do what I can to address the latest crisis. I'll find myself deciding on a plan without recognizing that the plan is going to require me to, essentially, add a full-time job to all the other things I have on my plate. But I don't notice that because I'm caught up in the passion of the moment. Over time, I've trained myself not to do that, but the impulse is still there. Maybe you can relate.

An essential piece of activism is being realistic about what you can and cannot do at this point in your life.

Be Steady with Your Energy

Radical realism demands that you look at the life you're living right now and determine what is doable for you. At this point in your life—your actual life, not the one you wish you were living or the life you feel you should be living, but your actual life—what are you capable of doing regularly? Are you the primary caregiver for young children or aging parents? That likely will mean you have less time available for your activist pursuits. Do you have a job that demands long hours? Are you dealing with health issues that affect your energy levels or your ability to move easily through the world? These will all impact your activist pursuits. Are you a student and school is your primary responsibility right now?

On the other side of the spectrum, maybe your kids are out of college and working in the world, taking care of themselves, and you now have more time than you've had in decades. Or perhaps you are retired and looking for meaningful work to engage in.

No matter where you are in your life journey, you need to be realistic about what you can and cannot do. What is sustainable at this point in your life? The old adage "Slow and steady wins the race" is true: When you are steady, you are more capable of honoring your abilities, your capacity, your timing, your rhythm, and your energy.

Realistically assess the responsibilities that are part of your everyday life and how much time and energy you have available once those commitments are met. This is where embracing the power of micro activism will save you. Micro activism allows you to do a small action that, when added to the actions of others, moves the world forward.

Assess Your Energy

▶ **Who is relying on me right now,** and how much of my time do I spend taking care of their needs?

▶ **Are there factors that impact my ability** to commit to a regular activist practice, for example, a disability, caring for small children, health issues, or financial pressures? Remember to be radically realistic here.

▶ **Are there ways that I can work around** these factors without overextending myself? For example, is there someone who could watch my kids for an hour a week so that I can help restock the shelves at our local food pantry? Or maybe I need to take on a task that I can do while the kids are napping, like writing post- cards to voters.

▶ **On any given day,** do I have a small chunk of time that I can dedicate to my activist work? Or is the truth that I'm pretty much at my maximum capacity with commitments? Again, we're talking about micro activism here. Doing an action that requires only 5 or 10 minutes of your time is absolutely worthwhile. Your answer here can be as simple as yes or no. If yes, think creatively about where you can find tiny bits of time to take an action.

Set Your Priorities

Let's look now at the question of where your chosen area of focus ranks in your priorities. If you're a parent (especially to a young child), and in school, and working a full-time job, you are not going to have a lot of capacity—and that is fine. What matters is that you accurately assess your capacity so that you don't overextend yourself, don't make promises that you can't keep, and don't set yourself up for failing both others and yourself. The saying "Under promise and over deliver" is so appropriate here. You want to fix things, and that is wonderful. At the same time, you have to be realistic about what you can and cannot do at any given time.

If you're experiencing a time crunch, what are some actions that you can realistically fit in to your schedule on a regular basis? MAKE A LIST.

Radical realism demands that you look at the life you're living right now and determine what is doable for you.

Lisa Brown

Seattle, Washington

What are you working toward?
Voting rights.

What motivates you?
My parents were activists, despite the cost to them professionally and personally. They lost their jobs and were investigated by the FBI. My father's Jewish heritage played into that reality. Now I realize that voting rights enable all sorts of other activism. Without that right, the struggles are harder and longer.

What does your work look like?
I am a fanatic postcard writer, sending postcards to people around the country reminding them to vote. My goal is to create a postcard that someone might want to hang on a refrigerator because it is fun to look at. If it is there on the refrigerator, maybe the date for registering, mailing a ballot, or going to the polls won't pass unnoticed. We are all so busy just trying to put one foot in front of the other, a little sunshine and color can really make a difference. Plus, the act of creating each card means something to me, I can pour a little of my creative self into projecting my hope to others.

How do you find and build community?
I am lucky to have a small community of activists where I live who help organize our group in support of voting rights and social justice. We are connected to larger organizations such as Reclaim Our Vote to make sure we are communicating to first-time voters or those who have only voted once before.

> **Every bit you do matters. Your goal to make two or three actions count every week, month, or year adds up over time.**

Who are your role models?
My first role model was my mother. She took me on a civil rights march when I was 10 years old, and it had a profound impact on me.

What keeps you going?
My superpower is grim persistence. It isn't glamorous, but it keeps me going.

What do you want to tell your future activist self?
Every bit you do matters. Your goal to make two or three actions count every week, month, or year adds up over time. I spent far too long thinking that a person had to do everything or might as well do nothing. Sometimes little things feel little, but they can add up to big things (and doing nothing is just unforgivable).

Do you have an intentional practice of self-care?
I have a regular yoga practice. Plus, I am a fiber artist and I spend time at my wheel spinning yarn, a form of meditation that works for my monkey brain.

Shallow Work vs. Deep Work

Our quick-fix culture tries to tell us that we can put a patch on something and that will be good enough. Sometimes something needs a quick patch, but we can't let it rest there and we shouldn't expect that the patch will fix the underlying problem. Quick fixes can make us feel like we've accomplished something, but they often mean we've kicked the can down the road for someone else to address.

If all we're ever doing is kicking the can down the road, then we are actually helping to maintain the systems that created the problem in the first place. For example, raising the national minimum wage would be a good accomplishment, but it would not address the larger issues of wealth inequality and generational cycles of poverty.

SHALLOW WORK UPHOLDS THE STATUS QUO

Shallow work is work that doesn't take the long view or consider nuances. Shallow work is often quick and flashy, and it supports oppressive systems. Shallow work is a distraction from the layers and complexities of the problems we're confronting, and it allows those systems to be maintained while it looks like we're making great strides. When we engage in shallow work, we're fooling ourselves and spinning our wheels.

We have to deliberately and intentionally take back our time and focus from the devices that are hijacking both. To make an impact in social justice work, or anywhere else for that matter, we need to be able to focus our attention for more than a few minutes at a time.

This is one reason I'm committed to my Noah's ark rule (page 52). Limiting yourself to one or, at most, two areas of focus and engagement can help you overcome the pull of surface-level instant gratification and cultivate the deep work that is required to change inequitable systems and to meaningfully address the challenges that we are facing.

For example, the climate crisis will not be remedied by throwing your empty plastic bottles into your recycling bin at home. In fact, the emphasis on recycling shifts the problem onto the consumer rather than the manufacturer. The manufacturer should be held responsible for addressing the problems of overusing natural resources, creating too much waste, and polluting the environment. Only about 10 percent of plastic is actually recycled. The majority is slowly breaking down in landfills to become microplastics, which are arguably more dangerous than the original products. When it comes to protecting the planet and to addressing climate change, recycling is just one tiny piece in a much larger mosaic. We must take the time and do the work to go beyond slogans and beyond actions that seem good but aren't as impactful as we might be led to believe.

Doing shallow work undermines real progress because we have the illusion that we are doing something that moves the needle a little bit, but in fact we aren't. This is how we can confuse liking a post on social media for activism. There's nothing wrong with liking a post; it's just not a substitute for real action. It is not a substitute for doing the hard work of gaining knowledge, building relationships, and taking thoughtful, intentional actions that support the overarching goal.

SHALLOW WORK TAKES TIME, TOO

The other thing about shallow work that's important to recognize is that it, too, takes time. Time is a limited resource, and if you're spending it doing shallow work, you are, unintentionally, upholding the systems you are committed to breaking down. There are only so many hours in a day, and hours spent on shallow work are stolen from hours that could be spent on deep work.

A good rule of thumb is to ask yourself, "What result, over the long term, will this action have?" If you can't see a positive benefit, then it's likely that the action you are doing is shallow work and your time would be better spent focusing on something more intentional.

Narrowing and deepening your focus allows you to take informed action and see how your micro activism fits in to the larger whole. It's like a 1,000-piece jigsaw puzzle: You might only hold one or two pieces in your hand, but the puzzle will never be complete without those pieces.

DOING DEEP WORK

Deep work can take a long time before producing results, but it disrupts oppressive systems. While big, successful actions are exciting and necessary, they aren't the norm—not even for Headliners. For the majority of people, finding small, regular, sustainable actions is the healthier, more realistic form of activism. Deep work identifies the overarching goal and then plots a path from here to there with small, meaningful actions leading the way.

Deep work breaks down systems that uphold an unjust status quo. Unlike shallow work, deep work gets to the heart of the problems we are confronting. Deep work looks at the nuances and the intersections with other systems of oppression and assesses the fundamental changes that need to be made in order to accomplish the ultimate goal. Deep work engages in probing, open-ended questions rather than binaries and quick-fix thinking.

Deep work requires critical thinking and encourages the expression of opposing viewpoints.

CONFLICT IS NOT NECESSARILY BAD

It's lovely when we can all agree on something, but in practice that often means one or more people are withholding their deeply held beliefs and wisdom so as to not create conflict within the group.

To do meaningful deep work, we have to get over the idea that conflict is inherently bad. It is through exploring

Are You Doing Deep Work?

▶ **Are there places** where the actions I am taking are more weighted toward shallow work than deep work?

▶ **If so, how can I shift** into deep work? What would deep work look like in my area of focus?

▶ **How can I break up** deep work into micro actions that I can commit to regularly—actions that are so small that not doing them seems silly, like a 2-minute call to my representative's office to express my support for a particular bill, writing one postcard to a voter, or pulling one can of food off my shelf to donate to the local food pantry?

▶ **What kind of celebratory traditions** can I create to acknowledge the progress I am making?

conflicting opinions and experiences that we broaden our perspective. For example, two people may grow up in middle-class families in the same city, but their experiences may differ if one is a person of color and the other is white. If we can examine those differing experiences, we can learn a lot about one another and the direction in which our activist work may need to go.

Cultivate Curiosity

Difficult conversations are part of activist work. The greatest tool we have at our disposal is curiosity. When we are curious about something, we are open to learning and expanding our understanding of the issue. Curiosity takes us away from worrying about ourselves and puts our attention on someone else and their life experience.

When you're feeling defensive about something someone is saying, a good practice is to get curious. Ask questions. Try to find out where they are coming from, and try to find places where you can relate to their experience, even if it is very different from your own.

Radical realism lets us proceed from a foundation of truth. It gets us out of the realm of "I should do this" and into "This is what I can honestly expect of myself." We stop setting our-selves up for failure based on unrealistic expectations, and in contrast, we create a habit of activism that we can sustain.

White Privilege and Activism

Some people misinterpret the term *white privilege* to mean that white people are to blame for the inequities in our world. No one alive now is responsible for creating the systems that we are struggling to dismantle. No one alive now should feel guilt for something they had no hand in creating. In addition, the existence of white privilege doesn't mean that white people do not experience difficulty in life. It simply means that having white skin doesn't make your life more difficult.

Here's an example from my own experience. When I'm in a store and need to put on my glasses so that I can read a label, I step back into the center of the aisle so as not to be accused of shoplifting as I put my hand in my bag. I do this automatically because of the experiences I have had in stores. My white friends do not do this.

White privilege is like inherited wealth—you have an advantage, but you didn't do anything to earn it, and you get to choose how to use it. Are you going to use your privilege to address the inequities in society? Or are you going to enjoy the benefits of it without acknowledging that racial inequity causes harm?

In activist work, every white person can use their privilege to help dismantle fundamentally unjust systems. If you have white privilege, use it. Let go of guilt, accept responsibility, and be curious. Feeling guilty about having white privilege is understandable, but guilt can be so paralyzing that it can prevent people from taking action. Accepting responsibility and using whatever privilege you have for good is empowering. If you are white, ask yourself: Where in my life does white privilege show up? How can I use my privilege to make a positive difference? How can I talk about white privilege with other white people to highlight the inherent inequities and our responsibility to make change?

If, instead, you are a person of color, ask yourself: How can I talk with white friends and colleagues about white privilege with the goal of getting them to use their privilege in service of those with less privilege without shaming or blaming?

Bob Norton

Bellingham, Washington

What goal are you working toward?

Waking up white cis men like me to start to understand patriarchy and racism, and to move the needle in the direction of dismantling both systems.

What motivates you?

My former wife, who identifies as BIPOC, was finally able to help me see my privilege and position. This was after three years of me taking part in antiracism training and learning through my workplace and church. Ignoring what is happening would be aiding fascists in their efforts to take power. I can choose to hide in my white male privilege, but at some point a decision has to be made as to where I stand, to maintain that privilege or not.

What does your work look like?

I invited white men into a four-month conversation about patriarchy and racism, while recovering (uncovering?) our vulnerability with/toward/for each other to build trust and have real, hard conversations.

How do you find and build community?

I invite several friends and acquaintances to gather outside on my deck once a week, so we had a community built around conversation and learned that none of us had really experienced intentional community.

I want to tell myself this is a marathon, not a sprint.

Who are your role models?
My ex-wife, my boss, a good friend who was practicing this work
for years before me; also bell hooks, Layla Saad, W. Kamau Bell,
and Omkari!

What keeps you going?
Remembering that it is my privilege to choose not to keep going
while many have no choice but to keep going: my daughter,
my sisters, my ex-wife, my friends, my coworkers, more than
half the world population.

What do you want to tell your future activist self?
I want to tell myself this is a marathon, not a sprint. And to
be kind to my friends and relatives who are slow to come around
to my point of view.

Do you have an intentional practice of self-care?
Daily meditation, massage, golf therapy, reading fiction.

Be Brave in Your Conversations

These are not easy subjects to discuss. We aren't always as adept at difficult conversations as we wish we were, yet the only way to create the world we want is to be willing to engage in challenging conversations. We must be willing to do the hard work of recognizing our own responsibility and our privilege, and then to use those realizations to inform the work we do. Dr. Robin DiAngelo writes more about these issues in her book *White Fragility*. I encourage you to read it, along with the books on race I have listed in the resources (page 171).

If you're feeling defensive about something someone is saying, a good practice is to get curious.

Chapter Takeaways

Practicing **RADICAL REALISM** helps you stay in the activist game.

CELEBRATING YOUR WINS, no matter how small, is essential.

Shallow work upholds oppressive systems, while **DEEP WORK** disrupts oppressive systems.

If you have **WHITE PRIVILEGE**, use it: Let go of guilt, accept responsibility for working to make change, and be curious.

↓
↓
↓

➡ We Need Other People

Western culture celebrates a go-it-alone philosophy. We revere the person who sets out on their own path and blazes a trail without help from anyone. The strong, quiet hero who is beholden to none. We're also led to believe that to add value to society, we have to create something new. While I respect the qualities of dedication and perseverance and innovation, there are aspects of this attitude that are detrimental.

You don't have to reinvent the wheel every time you set out to do something. You don't have to come up with a new way of doing something just for the sake of it being yours. There are many people already doing work in your area of activism with whom you can collaborate rather than compete.

↓
↓
↓

We are not meant to go it alone. We live in community with others. Even monks in the mountains of Tibet who have taken vows of silence are living in community. Ditching the go-it-alone mentality makes it much easier to engage in community with a sense of joy.

Community Offers Power

It's in community that we can find power: the power that comes from working with others to achieve a shared goal; the power that comes with numbers; the power that comes from refining our strategies and tactics in the clarifying fire of honest, courageous conversations. When we are focused on achieving a goal more than on being the first or the most successful, we expand our impact exponentially.

When we collaborate, we find ourselves in a structure that holds the potential to keep us going when times are tough. No goal of social change is accomplished without disappointments and setbacks. In fact, social change usually happens over a time frame of decades and centuries, not months. Given that change is hard-won and generally slow to achieve, working in community makes the struggle easier to bear and the wins even more satisfying to celebrate.

Determine What Community Looks Like for You

We often think of community as a physical community, people who share proximity. But there are also communities of ideas, of goals, of dreams—communities whose members may never physically meet but are connected by their shared commitments.

Sometimes a community that is built around a specific goal becomes a community for life.

---→

What a community looks like is for you to determine. Is it you and your closest friends and family all working toward a shared goal? Is it a large group of people who may never meet face-to-face but who have a shared cause that they are passionate about? You get to decide what your community looks like.

In addition to deciding how broad your community is, you get to decide how long you participate in it. Sometimes a community that is built around a specific goal becomes a community for life. At other times, once the goal is attained, the community disbands and members go on to other things.

How a community looks and how long it lasts should be based on the needs of the larger group, with each member determining their own place within it. Whatever your community looks like, it is undeniably true that community is where you will find strength in numbers and support—sometimes from the most unlikely sources.

START ONLINE

When you start to seek out community, it's easiest to start with the obvious places. If, for example, you're interested in the environment, look online for local groups that have the same interest. Unless your area of interest is obscure and specific, it's more than likely that there are people in your area working on the same thing. A quick internet search for "organizations near me doing climate change work" will often be enough to get you started.

If you're in a small town or a rural area, it might be hard to find people nearby with similar interests, but the online world means that no matter where you are, you can find community. You can find people to work with on the project(s) that are calling to you. I collaborate with people who live far from me all the time. We hop on to a video- or phone call and talk about what we're doing and strategies that we might employ, and we make sure that we're keeping each other going through challenging times. There are people I've yet to meet in person who are my primary community for various projects. We rely on each other's wisdom, commitment, and support.

ASK AROUND AND KEEP AN EYE OUT

Ask people if they're aware of anyone working in your area on the cause that you're committed to. You'd be surprised by the things people know that you don't think they know. We are all multifaceted and have areas of interest that are surprising to others. Take me as an example; I am a knitter and have long been concerned with how much clothing goes into landfills each year. I now know that many other people who knit have a strong interest in reducing the volume of wasted clothing. Finding that out was a surprise to me and a reminder of how many intersections exist that we are not aware of until we take the time to ask.

Check out the notice boards at your local coffee shop, community college, or health food store. People post notices for events that are happening around town, and you might stumble across the perfect thing if you're on the lookout for it. When I see something that looks interesting, I take a picture with my phone so that I don't have to worry about losing the information.

STAY OPEN TO SURPRISE

At one point, I found my community by going to one event. I had just moved from upstate New York to Savannah, Georgia, and I knew no one there, so I had legitimate concerns about becoming isolated. I made the decision to say yes to any invitation that was extended to me. A woman I met while getting the oil changed in my car told me about a group she thought I might find interesting, so I went.

I had low expectations, honestly, so I was pleasantly surprised to encounter a group of interesting and interested people. I went back the next week and the week after, and started to find my way into the community. There were people working on pretty much any aspect of social justice I could think of. And the range of people spanned the spectrum: people lacking financial resources and people with plenty of money; people with day jobs, family responsibilities, and health challenges. They all worked together, across lines that might otherwise have divided them, in service of the causes they were committed to.

FORM MULTIGENERATIONAL GROUPS

One of the things that stood out to me about the community in Savannah—and is a continued source of its strength—is that it is multigenerational. Whenever possible, I encourage you to have a broad age range in your group. People on both ends of the age spectrum have wisdom and perspectives to offer that are important for any group to incorporate into their planning and actions.

Savannah has some of the most skilled and dedicated activists I have ever met. I learned so much from them. Not only that, but I made friends I will cherish for the rest of my life. This is part of the power of working in community as an activist. There are pockets of people fighting for what is right all over the world, even in the most oppressive environments. They may not be readily visible, but if you look, you will find them. The support that you can provide one another is invaluable.

MEET A MICRO ACTIVIST

Precious Chika Musa

Boston, Massachusetts

What are you working toward?

Black liberation via commemorative practices that make room
for communal joy. Those practices include monument building
(and unbuilding), art exhibits and installations, and interrogating
who and how we memorialize our collective history of racialized
terror. I believe that by facing our past truthfully and honestly,
we can fill our present and future with unbridled joy.

What motivates you?

I believe my activism chose me. I'm a person who thrives when
my community thrives. And I hurt when my community hurts.
I identify as a Black feminist, and one of the building blocks of
Black feminism is an understanding of the intersecting nature
of an individual's identity. That means that our liberation is
interconnected. Since I'm not free, neither are you. Because I
want to be as I'm meant to be—free—and I'm committed to that
for myself and those who look like me. So, by extension, I'm
committed to that for you, whoever you are. In short, my love
for both of us motivates me.

What does your work look like?

A lot of listening and learning, especially when I enter new
spaces with new people who may or may not share similar
experiences to me. Outside of that practice, I work to create
artful spaces that center Black experiences and voices—as
complex and nuanced as they are.

How do you find and build community?

I went to Smith College, a women's college in Northampton,
Massachusetts. Smithies are radical people who do not stay

> I believe my activism chose me.
> I'm a person who thrives
> when my community thrives.

quiet about issues that concern them. My voice began there. The people who I raised my voice with are the people I still vibe with today. We think together, cry together, celebrate together. I tend to build community in academic spaces with folks who hold institutions accountable to their active and passive violence against the communities they traditionally keep in the margins. Academic spaces have connected me to local organizers and activists who have further connected me to artists and community members.

Who are your role models?
There are many, and I know I'm going to leave some out! But here we go. June Jordan, Tiara Austin, Ms. Lois D. Conley, De Nichols, Audre Lorde, Lucille Clifton, Alexis Pauline Gumbs, Salwa Abdussabur, Alana Woodson, Ogechi Musa.

What keeps you going?
Therapy! My bio family (especially my mama) and chosen family, my support stuffed animal (Spike), books, music, memory.

What do you want to tell your future activist self?
Girl, rest. Continue.

Do you have an intentional practice of self-care?
Exercise is really important to me, whether it's a really long walk, a light jog, boxing, dancing, or a workout. I need to move my body to remember I have a vessel to take care of who loves me and is deserving of love.

How to Find Your Community

▶ **What kind of community** am I looking for? In person, virtual, or both?

▶ **What focus** do I want the community to have? Specificity is necessary to be able to accomplish things consistently. For example, if the focus is on the environment, does the group work on plastic waste, water pollution, air pollution, renewable energy, or some other aspect?

▶ **What are the essential shared values** I want to find in this community? Is there, for example, a commitment to diversity, and respect for LGBTQIA+ people? Do we share a value of confidentiality within the group so that people feel safe bringing all of themselves to the community?

▶ **What do I want to get out** of being in this community beyond the satisfaction of doing the work? It's okay to desire something in addition to achieving your activist goal. If you want to find people you can talk with, or a regular place to show up and do the work, that's fine. You are allowed to want to fulfill other aspects of your life.

Allow Yourself to Learn from Others

One obstacle you may confront in your activist work is your own ego. Nobody likes to be seen as ignorant, yet ignorance is just a lack of knowledge; it can be corrected. Our culture turns healthy self-awareness into a challenge with an attitude of "Fake it till you make it." Trying to fake knowledge or competency when you don't have it actually cuts you off from the wisdom that is available out there. If we're all busy faking it, it's really hard to also be listening and learning.

While being willing to say "I don't know" can be hard, it's also liberating. You don't have to pretend; you can come to something as a beginner and learn from those farther down the path than you are. You can allow yourself to make mistakes without punishing yourself for being human. Where did we all get the idea that making a mistake is so bad? Mistakes, while often uncomfortable, are part of being human. The sooner you make the decision not to let discomfort deter you from working toward your goals, the sooner you will be able to truly open yourself to the learning that is possible when you set aside your ego.

MISTAKES ARE PART OF THE PROCESS

We can get particularly anxious about unintentionally causing harm to people with marginalized identities. For example, maybe you unintentionally used a term that is offensive, or you enacted a microaggression or some other hurtful behavior. It can be difficult to navigate these events. If we start from the understanding that we are all learning and that some of what we have been taught in the past is actually not okay, then we create space to learn from our mistakes, forgive ourselves, and, if we were on the receiving end of the harm, forgive those who unintentionally harmed us.

When we are learning a new skill or coming to a new understanding, we expect to make mistakes. For learning to occur, we have to be willing to be corrected when we have made a mistake or done harm, and willing to extend to ourselves the grace that we would extend to others. The grace that recognizes that the harm was unintentional. Rather than calling someone out, we can call them *in*—in to our experience of what they said or did—and allow them the opportunity to make amends.

We can do the same for ourselves. When we allow others to call us in, we are able to learn from our errors, apologize, and do better the next time. Shunning someone for a mistake gets us nowhere, and neither does beating ourselves up when we transgress. There is no learning without mistakes. Showing ourselves and others grace in our social justice work (and life in general) will free us from a lot of unnecessary suffering. Keeping a generous, open heart in our communities gets us further along than scorekeeping does.

EVERYONE HAS SOMETHING TO TEACH

Allowing ourselves to learn from others also means recognizing that pretty much everyone we meet has something to teach us. The more we can approach activism with what Buddhists call "beginner's mind"—staying open to learning and recognizing that we don't know everything (or maybe much at all)—the easier it will be to make the impact we want to make. We won't be spending our time and energy on proving how woke, committed, or special we are. We'll be doing the work in partnership with others, and with the intention of moving the needle toward justice in our area of focus.

I find it helpful to ask questions like the following: Who might have a different perspective on our way of working that might improve on how and what we're doing? Who might know the perfect person to help us with a challenge? Who might have resources that would benefit our work? Who might benefit from resources that we have? What collaborations are possible that we hadn't considered?

Wisdom lives in both those who have been at this work a long time and those new to it. It's up to us to be open to the wisdom that presents itself, no matter the messenger.

Share Your Wisdom

The other side of gathering wisdom is sharing it with others. I love the old saying "The best way to really learn something is to teach it to someone else." Who is coming along behind you who you can teach what you have learned?

To share wisdom in powerful ways requires humility. You must be willing to acknowledge that you are part of a long line of activists, and that the wisdom you have acquired is part of the work of more people than you will ever know or be able to thank. I think it's important to give credit to the source of my knowledge. It's as simple as letting people know "I read this in a book" or "I heard Jane say this." When I give credit where it's due, I am reminded of those who have come before and those who are doing the work now. I am also reminded that I am part of a larger whole.

How you share your wisdom depends on who you are. If your activist archetype is the Headliner, then standing on a stage and giving a talk may be the perfect way to share what you've learned. If your archetype is the Producer, a one-to-one mentor/mentee relationship might feel best. For the Organizer, perhaps leading a small group in studying your issue might be the way to go. And if you're an Indispensable, you may find that pulling together educational materials and disseminating them to the group feels most comfortable.

For any archetype, the most powerful wisdom is shared with humility. It's not about telling someone that you know the way. When you share what you've learned from the perspective that it might be just one of many ways of moving toward a goal, this has the most impact. Know-it-alls in activist work are just as unpopular as they are anywhere else.

Coco Guthrie-Papy

Savannah, Georgia

What are you working toward?

I pour my focus into criminal/juvenile justice work, reproductive justice, and voter's rights.

What motivates you?

Direct experience is a lot of it. Trying to access reproductive care, specifically abortion care in the South. Seeing people I love getting snagged by and drawn in to the criminal justice system. I think most people's activism is a combination of lived experience and the stories of those around them.

What does your work look like?

My goal is to have a society that works for everyone, a culture that doesn't define worth on proximity to wealth or whiteness or able-bodiedness. My default position is recognizing a problem, shedding light as to why it's a problem, and pushing back until that problem is solved. Since progress rarely moves at the urgency it deserves and rarely functions in a straight line, it becomes about noting the small wins, the work of the journey as much as the end results.

Who are your role models?

Grace Lee Boggs, Anne Braden, Septima Clarke, the Grimké sisters, James Baldwin, Georgia Gilmore. Also, the people around me. I have worked with some amazing activists and organizers in Savannah and from all over Georgia and the South.

> Love isn't about what we did yesterday; it's about what we do today and tomorrow and the day after.

What keeps you going?

There hasn't ever been a time in this country where the social conditions weren't hard. I often hear that "hope is a muscle," and that commonality is our connection. Grace Lee Boggs has a quote I live by: "We are beginning to understand that the world is always being made fresh and never finished; that activism can be the journey rather than the arrival; that struggle doesn't always have to be confrontational but can take the form of reaching out to find common ground with the many others in our society who are also seeking ways out from alienation, isolation, privatization, and dehumanization by corporate globalization." Love isn't about what we did yesterday; it's about what we do today and tomorrow and the day after.

What would you tell your activist self from 10 years ago?

Focus less on being "right." If you are trying to win hearts and minds, it's not about being right in your way; it's about meeting people where they are and finding a way for them to hear what you are saying. Show up for people. Take care of yourself. If you don't take care of yourself, your work will suffer, your relationships will suffer, you will suffer. This work is too important to burn yourself down. Find a way for this work to be a part of the type of life you don't have to escape from.

Build Bridges

It's human nature to want to hang out with people who share your beliefs and values. Communities are often constructed around broad identities such as liberal, progressive, or conservative politics. There are religious communities and professional communities. But we can also build communities around specific shared interests that connect groups that might otherwise be in opposition to one another. We can build collaborations with people with whom we share almost nothing, and these unlikely collaborations can have remarkable results.

For example, in 2018, liberal and conservative lawmakers in the United States decided to work together toward a shared goal of making reforms to the prison system. These people, whose ideologies were generally opposed, all wanted to reduce incarceration rates. Their reasons for advocating for policy change were very different, but the goal was the same. It was a most unlikely group, yet they put aside their ideological differences to work on this shared goal, and they were successful in passing the First Step Act, which led to the release of 20,000 people from prison.

Be a Pragmatist, Not a Purist

Many people, on all sides of any issue, are purists who only want to work with those who share their entire ideology. When we choose that route, we are cutting ourselves off from potentially powerful collaborations. If you and I share the goal of criminal justice reform, then the fact that we disagree on reproductive rights shouldn't be a deal breaker. This is not the purist view; it's the pragmatist view. If my goal is to get as many people as possible out of prison as quickly as possible and that's your goal, too, then that's what I'm going to focus on, even though you and I may disagree on issues outside of that.

We can build collaborations with people with whom we share almost nothing, and these unlikely collaborations can have remarkable results.

◀---

Who knows? Maybe our willingness to work together on one issue will reveal common ground on other issues. Being a purist is a luxury I don't believe we have in these times.

Finding common ground can require thinking outside the box. We have to pay attention to the words and actions of those who are not our natural allies. In the example of prison reform, lawmakers on the political right came at the issue from the perspective of believing in redemption; they were not seeing the opportunity for second chances in our system. Those on the political left were looking at the history of racism that runs through the prison system. Different perspectives, but one goal they rallied around. That there were different "whys" mattered less than the shared "what." They built a coalition that was able to make a meaningful start on their goal.

Look for Intersections

When you think more broadly about what other groups your activist cause intersects with, you position yourself to increase the impact of your micro actions by working in community with other people dedicated to other causes. Maybe your activist work is on climate change, with a particular focus on oceans and waterways. That intersects nicely with a group

↓
↓
↓

Stepping back and taking a wider view opens you up to collaborations that you might never have imagined.

--→

that is focused on sustainable farming practices. A group focused on reproductive rights will share many concerns with a group focused on reducing sexual assault. Is mental health your activist issue? If so, there is a direct intersection with criminal justice.

Stepping back and taking a wider view opens you up to collaborations that you might never have imagined and, consequently, to possibilities you might never have envisioned. And, even greater than that, finding intersections serves as a reminder that we are all connected. As Audre Lorde put it, "I am not free while any woman is unfree, even when her shackles are very different from my own." Lorde's wisdom applies to all of us. No one is truly free until we all are free. Your cause may not be my cause, yet because the goal of all our causes is freedom, your cause belongs to me and mine to you, because we are both part of the human family.

One of the best parts of being in a community is that our communities are sources of support for us both as individuals and as organizations. Our communities are our activist home. Home, hopefully, is where we go to rest, restore, and reconnect with ourselves both in our activist pursuits and in the rest of our life.

How to Find Collaborative Partners

▶ **Is there a group** that seems to oppose my general perspective but that shares my activist concern?

▶ **What benefits might I get** from a collaboration with this group? Make a list of possible benefits—for example, increased public awareness of the issue, or media coverage as two typically opposing groups form a coalition.

▶ **Do I want to consider reaching out** to an opposing group and discussing how working together around this specific issue might get both of us something we want?

Chapter Takeaways

A GO-IT-ALONE ATTITUDE is more likely to keep you isolated and struggling than to lead to meaningful change.

COMMUNITY helps when times are tough and gives you people with whom to celebrate your wins.

YOU GET TO DECIDE what community means to you: small, large, in-person, or virtual.

Practice **BEGINNER'S MIND** and allow yourself to learn from others.

We all make mistakes; **BE HUMBLE**, apologize, and do better going forward.

EXTEND GRACE to those who make mistakes, including yourself.

SHARE YOUR WISDOM, build bridges, and look for intersections.

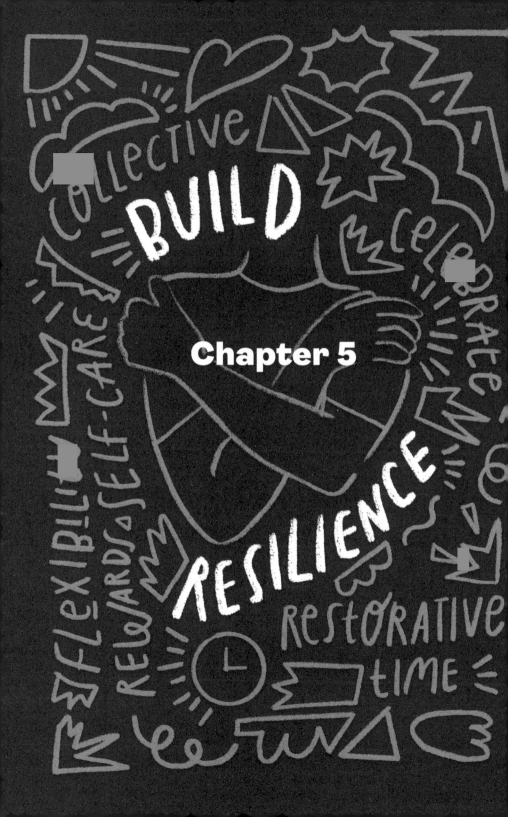

Chapter 5

BUILD RESILIENCE

COLLECTIVE

CELEBRATE

FLEXIBILITY

SELF-CARE

REWARDS

RESTORATIVE TIME

→ Staying Strong over the Long Haul

One of the most important things to do if you are going to stay in the work of change-making is to build resilience. I think about resilience a lot, in relation not just to activism but also to my life as a whole. The Covid-19 pandemic was a test of resilience, for us as individuals and also for our systems. The weaknesses in our systems became clear, but so did our personal strength.

We often equate resilience with being tough, and we equate toughness with not caring, but it's important to recognize that resilience is not the absence of caring. In fact, the ability to care deeply and find your strength at the same time is the hallmark of a truly resilient person.

It helps to recognize that people are often more resilient than they think they are. If life has ever dealt you a blow that really hurt, you might have been knocked down for a bit. But if you still show up to make the change that you can, resilience is part of who you are.

In this chapter I will share some tools that will help you become more resilient. Remember, the primary strategy is one that many people have a hard time with: the Noah's ark rule (page 52). Limit your activist work to one or, at most, two areas of focus. This will truly help you stay in the activist game. Let's also look at how to reduce (or, better yet, avoid) emotional overload, that feeling of "If I have to do another thing my brain will explode." And let's look at how to address burnout, that feeling of "I've done too much and now I'm fried."

Avoid Getting Overwhelmed

If you want to be effective as an activist, you have to be able to sustain your work over long periods, often, seemingly, without much to show for your efforts. In a world that tells us to "go for the gold," and in which "loser" is one of the worst things you can be called, it's easy to fear failure.

Maybe you set a big goal and don't recognize the dozens of incremental steps that it will take to achieve that goal. In such a case, you might become so focused on the big win that you don't notice the small accomplishments along the way.

Or maybe you neglect to ask for help—or you refuse to accept help that is offered—because you feel that a project rests on you and that receiving help means you've somehow failed to do your part.

Or, in still other situations, maybe you take on more than makes sense, given the other responsibilities you have in life. Maybe you've forgotten that "Fake it till you make it" isn't the best path to a goal and that acknowledging what you don't know isn't shameful. Or maybe you're in a leadership position and have a hard time delegating because you feel that you should be shouldering more of the responsibility.

Whatever the reason, when you choose not to recognize the actual limits of your capacity, you are setting yourself up for emotional overload and its trusty companion, burnout.

Remember That You Are Not Alone

The most crucial element in building your resilience is to employ radical realism. As I've mentioned, your capacity is not unlimited, and you have to know what is and isn't possible for you at any given moment. Part of maintaining resilience is acknowledging that, in whatever area of activism you have chosen, you are not alone. When you need to pull back and take a break, or say no to another task, others will pick up the slack. "But," you might say, "what if there *is* no one else to do something?" If you're following the path of micro activism, that shouldn't be the case: The whole point is to take small, sustainable actions on a regular basis.

However, if you've fallen off the micro action wagon and back into the "Go big or go home" trap, then you have a choice to make. If what you're doing is time-sensitive, you have to determine whether you can delegate the task to someone else or whether you can push through with the understanding that you are going to need downtime to recover on the other side.

And I suggest that, after delegating or taking that downtime, you look at reworking your plan so that you have more support, or scale back so that your commitment is truly sustainable for you. It is better to stay out of emotional overload and burnout than to recover from them.

Reduce Decision Fatigue

Decision fatigue is what we experience when we must make a decision and there are too many options. I experience this even when doing something as simple as looking at a huge menu at a restaurant. I don't want to sit there and struggle to decide what I want. I want a curtailed menu that I can easily decipher.

Some successful people decide that the fewer mundane choices they have to make, the better, so they choose a kind of uniform, essentially wearing the same thing every day: Steve Jobs's black turtleneck and jeans, Hillary Clinton's signature pantsuits, Ellen DeGeneres's blazer and button-down. You don't necessarily have to limit your wardrobe, but the principle behind choice reduction is significant.

When you limit yourself to one or two areas of focus in your activism, you reduce decision fatigue. The fewer decisions you have to make, the more you can focus your efforts. When you focus your efforts, the more likely you are to take consistent action and the easier it is to make activism a regular part of day-to-day life.

In the process of writing this book, I gave myself a schedule. This is not how I normally operate. Of course, I schedule meetings with clients and podcast interviews, but I don't typically set a schedule for tasks that involve only me. However, I knew that not giving myself a writing schedule was a sure setup for having to pull all-nighters to meet the deadline (and I was terrible at all-nighters in college). So I made a plan. Five days a week I would get up at 6:30 a.m., practice yoga, write in my journal, have some coffee, do the daily crossword puzzle, shower, and dress. That allowed me to be at my desk at 9:00 a.m.

That was the plan, and it wasn't negotiable. After writing until 10:30, I'd take a short break and then go back at it until at least noon. Proof that my plan worked? Here you are, holding my book. The plan worked because it eliminated decision fatigue. I did not have to decide what time to sit down at my desk in the morning; that decision had been made—9:00 a.m. And I only had to stay at my desk until noon. I didn't try to write for eight hours a day. That was never going to happen. Admittedly, the first week was a bit hard, because I hadn't worked with that kind of routine since college, but sticking to my schedule built stamina and resilience. Also, I had a great sense of satisfaction at the end of each writing session.

Incorporate Restorative Time

Another reason my plan worked was that I built in restorative time. Once noon arrived, I was free to continue writing if I was on a roll, move on to other work, or shut down my computer and do something else entirely. My plan was structured to make resilience part of it. My plan factored in that there were other things that would need doing, and that there is a limited amount of time that anyone can do any kind of demanding work before reaching the point of diminishing returns.

The more you can plan your activist work as a regular part of your life, the better able you will be to create systems that sustain it. If you sign up for a shift at the food bank every Thursday, that's your schedule; the fatigue that comes with decision-making is taken out of the process. There is a reason that most of us buy the same toothpaste and dish soap again and again: What we've selected meets our needs, and we don't find ourselves standing in the aisle at the grocery store for

10 minutes trying to decide which toothpaste we're going to get every time; we know, we grab, we go.

It's the same with activism: If you meet with your team of people working for reproductive rights on Tuesdays at 10:00 a.m., then you don't have to make a decision about the day and time; you also have the benefit of knowing that, at least on Tuesday mornings, you have people to talk with about the challenges and frustrations that you are experiencing as you do your activist work.

Systematize to Eliminate Obstacles

Another thing that can get in your way are obstacles in your own systems. The more you can systematize the things that you do regularly, the better. Having on hand the materials you need for regular tasks—printer paper, contact info, art supplies, coffee, or whatever else you normally require to do your work—reduces the likelihood of being derailed. You won't have to spend time looking for supplies rather than doing your activist work. Part of building resilience is reducing the number of obstacles you face that distract you from staying in action around the cause you care about.

What are some systematic obstacles that get in the way of doing your activist work? For example, you regularly need the contact information for your state and local legislators. Do you have to look it up every time? Or suppose your team doesn't have regular task assignments. Who's going to restock the coffee? Think for a while about ways to eliminate such obstacles.

Do the Most Good

Let me be very clear here: When I talk about maximizing your impact, I am not talking about doing huge actions. I'm talking about taking your micro actions and leveraging them so that they do the most good possible.

Let's say that your micro action is giving a meal to an unhoused person in your neighborhood every week. Rather than randomly giving meals to anyone who is unhoused, consider giving to the same person each week. This would allow you to accomplish a couple of things: First, you can build a relationship with that person; you get to know their story, and they get to know yours. Second, you become a point of stability in what is often a chaotic situation; knowing that there is a meal coming could free up the person to do something that might help move them out of their current situation.

Perhaps your micro action is writing postcards to voters around the country, encouraging them to participate in local elections. Are you gifted with abilities that you can use to make your postcards eye-catching works of art likely to spur the recipient to vote?

Maybe you write a regular newsletter updating people in your community on what is happening regarding an issue of concern in your town. If you send it to your local paper as a letter to the editor, you might widen the circle of people aware of that issue.

I recommend brainstorming about impact maximization with other people. It can be hard for us to see where we can expand our efforts; often people with a bit more distance will have great ideas.

Make Micro Actions Part of Your Daily Life

Making micro activism a regular part of your life not only takes decision fatigue out of the picture but also has the benefit of building your capacity. The more you do, the more you can do, the more you learn, and the better able you are to contribute to the cause that has your heart.

What are some ways you can work a micro action into your life every day? For example, if you're collaborating with a group to help unsheltered people, you might make a small care package on Monday, send an email to an elected official on Tuesday, talk with one person about joining your group on Wednesday, Thursday can be for collecting gently worn items from the friends you emailed last week, and Friday can be for dropping off those things at the weekly meeting.

The Real Point of Self-Care

When we think about self-care, a lot of people think about things like getting a massage or a manicure. Now, I will never say no to a good pedicure, but that isn't the highest meaning of self-care. The concept of self-care has been commodified and sold to us in various ways, telling us we should care for ourselves individually rather than considering the well-being of the whole. While caring for our bodies is certainly part of self-care, being told that self-care is only about our individual bodies and that it is something we buy (accessible only to those who have money to spend on it) misses the real point.

The point of self-care isn't that it feels good; it's that self-care builds resilience. True self-care expands our capacity to respond to the things that are challenging in our lives. True self-care encompasses our body, mind, and spirit and allows us to experience ourselves as connected to the larger whole. True self-care happens when we take care of *us*, the individual and the collective: our families, our friends, our neighbors and coworkers, our towns, our villages, our cities, our planet.

Activist work makes demands on all elements of us; true self-care restores what is depleted in doing the work of making meaningful change.

SELF-CARE CAN BE MANY THINGS

Is it time with friends or family that reconnects you to your support system? Is it time alone with a good book (or a trashy summer read) that gives you space to unwind? Perhaps it's time spent in nature that reminds you that you are part of a beautiful world. Or maybe it's a couple of days away from home during which the only person you have to please is yourself. Is there a hobby that you love? When you're engaged in it, does the rest of the world fall away, leaving you in a groove of focus and joy?

For some people, self-care means diving in to a hard project that uses an entirely different part of their brain than their regular work does. For instance, if you work as an activist and your career is all about engaging with people, then a project like building a model plane from a kit might be the quiet, solo activity that your soul is calling for. Alternatively, if you are working from home and alone most of the day, a part of self-care might look like going out with a few friends and socializing with other humans.

CARE OF THE COLLECTIVE

At the same time, we don't want to leave out the element of larger connection. We do not live on this planet alone. We cannot separate our well-being from the well-being of others and expect to achieve meaningful change. Reframing self-care as activities that allow us not only to feel better in our own bodies but also to contribute to the care of the collective self will do more for us than separating ourselves from the rest of humanity. For some people, time working at a soup kitchen or writing to incarcerated people is an act of self-care.

Find the thing, or combination of things, that restores your body, mind, and soul so that you can keep doing the work you are doing. Find the combination that allows you to bring the best of you to all the parts of your life. Find what reinforces your connection to being an integral part of this world rather than an isolated individual just getting through

↓
↓
↓

the day. Identifying what feeds you and what makes you feel connected to the larger whole, and making time to bring at least some of those elements into your life on a regular basis, is key to being able to sustain yourself through hard times. Whether other people think of it as self-care or not doesn't matter; that's why the word *self* is in there. Self-care is what you decide it is for you.

SELF-CARE CAN EVOLVE

Self-care, like life, is always changing. What works at one point in your life may not be what is best at another. If you have young children who need a great deal of time and attention, then self-care may be heavily weighted toward rest so that you have the capacity to fulfill your various roles. When evaluating what self-care might look like for you right now, consider what is missing from your life: sufficient rest, more stimulation, time to read a book for fun, nourishing food, time with friends and family? What haven't you been getting that you need? Bring that into your self-care.

One of my self-care tools while writing this book was to take a short nap around 3:00 p.m. By that point in the day, I felt like I could fall asleep standing up, so why fight it? I took 20 to 30 minutes of sleep, and I felt refreshed and ready to move into the rest of the day. I know that the idea of napping can be odd for those of us who live in cultures where it is not a common practice, but there's a reason that some cultures take a break midway through the day. It's not just about the afternoon heat; it's also about paying attention to how the human body works. There's nothing wrong with the afternoon coffee you're craving, but be aware that your brain is telling you it needs a break. You can override that with caffeine, but what you truly need is a bit of rest. If it's possible for you to take even 10 minutes and put your head down on your desk, I promise you it's more energizing than coffee, and the coffee is still there if you want it.

What Is Your Self-Care?

- ▶ **What does self-care** currently look like for me?

- ▶ **How might I make** my self-care more nourishing?

- ▶ **Would I benefit** from creating more structure in my life? Or would less structure work best for me at this time?

- ▶ **What is currently missing** from my daily life that would be nourishing to include? For example, alone time if you're constantly with people, people time If you spend the bulk of your days alone, analog time if you're on a device all day, or a hobby that uses a different part of your brain than your work calls for.

- ▶ **Would it help me** to bring a friend into my self-care (for example, scheduling regular walks or check-in calls)? If so, who?

- ▶ **Is there an element of support** for the collective that would make my self-care more nourishing for me (for example, time spent tutoring a child, or working in the community garden)?

Michelle Solomon

Savannah, Georgia

What goal are you working toward?

Participation. I work in a lot of different subject areas, but underlying it all, I want to help people be informed and involved with what's going on in their community.

What motivates you?

The clerical, technical, maintenance, and cafeteria workers at my college went on strike my senior year at Yale University. I had come from a privileged background, and the power imbalance between the very rich university and its lowest-paid workers was eye-opening, as was the way those workers were able to claim power and negotiate. Later, I trained with the AFL-CIO as a labor organizer and worked as a tenant organizer and a community organizer in various capacities.

What does your work look like?

There's a real difference between being a paid organizer vs. organizing around issues I care about in my own community, and it's always a complicated choice about how much of a leadership role to take. I know that I have never successfully accomplished anything on my own. It's always about putting together a team and sharing responsibility.

How do you find and build community?

It's always relationships. Always. I find people who are excited about something that I'm excited about, and we come up with ideas of how we could work on that thing, we make a plan, and we do the thing.

Who expects anything to be easy?
Especially social change in the South.
I have realistic expectations
about what's achievable and choose
actions accordingly.

Who are your role models?
It's more teachers than role models. When I was a young organizer, there were people who taught me how to organize. Some of it was formal training, and some of it was hands-on experience.

What keeps you going?
Well, I'm a Jew, and I maintain a healthy dose of cynicism at all times. Who expects anything to be easy? Especially social change in the South. I have realistic expectations about what's achievable and choose actions accordingly. Being realistic about power helps to prevent heartbreak. Being Jewish informs my understanding of the world, my place in it, my responsibility, how problems get solved, my sense of what is just, how we construct meaning, how society is organized, and how power works. Though I'm not particularly observant, I have a profoundly Jewish worldview. This saying especially resonates with me: "It is not your responsibility to finish the work of perfecting the world, but you are not free to desist from it either," Rabbi Tarfon (Pirkei Avot 2:21).

What do you want to tell your future activist self?
Indulge yourself sometimes—travel, eat at a good restaurant—it's okay to spend money on yourself just for fun.

Do you have an intentional practice of self-care?
Long walks with the dog every day. Trashy, trashy novels, and lots of them. And I watch reality TV with my kid, too. Let myself take days off when I feel like it. Working for myself rocks.

↓
↓
↓

Leave Room for Flexibility

We've all encountered (or perhaps been, at times) people who are so rigid in their habits that the slightest change sends them into a tailspin. Things have to be done in a specific way, or everything falls apart. (To be clear, I'm not talking about people with diagnosed conditions.) That might work when we are doing things that require no input from anyone else, but it doesn't work when we are engaging with other humans. And, honestly, it's a hard way to live. Life throws unexpected things at us all the time, and developing a tolerance for the unexpected and a willingness to be flexible will serve us well and increase our resilience.

A key part of resilience is being able to adapt to changing circumstances. When opportunities present themselves, we need to be flexible to see where we can use them to serve our cause. When laws change, we need to adapt our actions to work within them, peacefully refuse to abide by them, or change course to align our actions with our principles of equity and justice.

Flexibility allows us to see things from different perspectives and to come up with solutions that we might otherwise miss, like finding common ground on an issue with someone with whom we otherwise share little.

We challenge ourselves and the organizations we're engaged with to keep evolving and growing when we consider where we might be more flexible and still be aligned with our values. Taking a look at the bigger picture gives us opportunities to stretch ourselves—and the ability to stretch ourselves is a key part of resilience. Skyscrapers are constructed to be flexible so that they can withstand strong winds.

Find Your Flexibility

▶ **Where have I been flexible in my activist work,** and what benefits have I gained?

▶ **Where have I (or my group) been afraid to change,** and how has that gotten in the way of progress?

▶ **What are three areas where more flexibility might pay off?** For example, soliciting the input of others, especially those older or younger; changing my routine just to see what happens; or reaching out to a group to see where we might find common ground.

↓
↓
↓

Mindy Tsonas Choi

Newburyport, Massachusetts

What goal are you working toward?

My work is to build collective belonging. By reframing belonging through a collective lens instead of an individual one, we dismantle how capitalist structures divide, disenfranchise, and commodify people. Collective belonging, as a strategy and framework, is inherently humanizing, connective, reparative, and regenerative.

What motivates you?

As a transracial Korean American adoptee who was separated from my birth family and country of origin, I feel as though I have always been on a quest for belonging. My personal search, alongside my growth and learning in community as an activist, led me to seek a much broader understanding of belonging through a more critical lens.

What does your work look like?

Primarily, it's about facilitating ways we can strengthen and build relationships, especially across barriers of division. Changing the script toward collective belonging means telling new stories of interconnection to interrupt beliefs that uphold belonging as an ideology of individualism, scarcity, and exclusivity.

How do you find and build community?

As an artist and storyteller, I use the creative process as a playful and accessible way to bring people together and have meaningful interactions. Through making things together and sharing stories of diverse lived experiences, we witness one another's humanity. Much of my community building is done through facilitating small circles of confluence and care, often disguised as an art project.

Much of my community building is done through facilitating small circles of confluence and care, often disguised as an art project.

Community art projects offer us a tangible way forward together, showing us what is possible when we work with shared purpose.

Who are your role models?

Much of how I came to understand collective belonging, as a foundational organizing principle, was through adrienne maree brown's work of emergent strategy. I'm also inspired by the work of Grace Lee Boggs for how she championed community and modeled collective organizing. Eugene Lee Yang is a favorite Korean American artist and activist doing necessary collective work, smashing binaries and queering culture in his own beautiful way.

What keeps you going?

I try to remember that my work is not about me. When I embrace my own collective experience, I immediately feel more grounded, supported, and less alone.

What would you want to tell your younger activist self?

First, I would tell my younger self that you belong, and that it was always the systems that said otherwise. Then I would say, "You don't need to push so hard." Activism doesn't have to look a certain way or happen at a certain intensity or pace to create meaningful change.

Do you have an intentional practice of self-care?

Reframing care as collective, relational, and interconnected—because none of us exist in a vacuum, and all our actions have direct and indirect impact—gives us greater access to regeneration and healing that allows all of us to thrive. Care for self is care for everyone around us.

↓
↓
↓

Celebrate Your Wins

Okay, tell the truth: How often do you celebrate the wins that you have? Not just in your activist life but in life in general? Do you give yourself a little internal high five when you manage to park your car in a tiny space the first try? Do you get donuts (make mine jelly, please) for the group after a successful presentation at work? Do you have a celebratory meal after getting an A in a class or getting positive feedback from your boss about a big project you've been working on?

Most of us just keep on moving past our wins without taking the time to acknowledge that we just accomplished something. If we were in the car with a friend who accomplished parking magic, we'd say, "Nice job!" But when it's our own achievements, we can be very stingy with the celebration. Here's the thing: Celebrating your wins not only feels good in the moment but is also a great way to keep yourself motivated over the long term. You'll remember those wins when things get hard, and the possibility of more of them won't seem quite so remote.

If you're only paying attention to what's going wrong, it's pretty hard to stay in the game. I'm a huge tennis fan, and something that I've noticed when I'm watching a doubles match is that even if someone makes a couple of bad serves and costs their team a point, their teammate is right there with a fist bump or some other encouragement. Of course, they aren't saying "Great job" at a mistake, but they are saying "I believe in you—you'll get it next time." And when their teammate does do something great, they are right there to acknowledge the success.

I think this is such a good model. We are practicing radical realism on both ends of the spectrum when we mark the wins as much as we note the losses.

How to Mark Small Successes

What are some ways you can celebrate wins both small and large? Some of my celebratory actions are going to my favorite bakery and buying a cookie that I love but generally don't indulge in, taking a long bath with a glass of wine while I watch a movie, or going out for a meal. For a really big accomplishment, I take a couple of days away. You might indulge in an extra-long walk, a conversation with a friend in which you toot your own horn, a trip to a museum that you love but rarely visit, time in a bookstore where you can wander with no agenda, or maybe a date night with your partner. What you do does not matter; it's the fact that you acknowledge and celebrate small successes.

Make a list of things that would feel good to treat yourself to after a win.

Now commit to acknowledging your wins aloud. Better yet, pick something from your list to celebrate the wins that come along and treat yourself right.

Chapter Takeaways

Reduce **EMOTIONAL OVERLOAD** by maintaining your focus on one or two areas of activism.

EDUCATE YOURSELF ABOUT YOURSELF: Self-knowledge is power.

REDUCE DECISION FATIGUE.

MAXIMIZE YOUR IMPACT not by doing more, but by leveraging what you are doing to get the most from your efforts.

PRACTICE SELF-CARE, including care for the collective self.

Leave room for **FLEXIBILITY.**

CELEBRATE YOUR WINS.

↓
↓
↓

Chapter 6

WHAT'S YOUR LEGACY?

LISTEN

OPENNESS

MEANINGFUL

CONNECTION
TEACHING

ASK

→ Legacy Encompasses Past, Present, and Future

When I think of legacy as something handed down from the past, it connects me to the present moment in ways that surprise me. I say *surprise* because we often think about legacy in terms of objects or long-term projects that are passed from generation to generation. But our actions each day are part of the legacy we leave.

When I was living in Savannah, I read a news article about a woman who always gave money to anyone on the street who asked her for it. She wasn't a wealthy person and couldn't give a lot, but she always gave something. That really struck me, and I decided I would give it a try. Typically, days would go by when I wouldn't encounter anyone asking for money, but—as these things often happen—once I made that decision I was presented with an opportunity to see if I'd meant it.

It was August, which means it was ungodly hot in Savannah. I was in my car at a stoplight when a man approached asking for spare change. Thinking how odd it was that this opportunity presented itself the same day I read the article about the woman, I rolled down my window and gave him a couple of dollars. As I did, I saw the guy in front of me get out of his truck, grab a bottle of water from the back, and hand it to the man along with some money. The man receiving the money and water was so grateful, I think as much to be seen as a fellow human as for the money and water. I found myself on the verge of tears. The three of us had been witness to and participants in our shared humanity. It was a profound moment. We had each left a small legacy of hope, decency, and care with people we didn't know and would likely never see again. It's been years since that happened, and the feeling of connection and gratitude is still very strong in my body. That's the power of leaving an intentional legacy.

Legacy Doesn't Have to Be about Big Actions

Most of us want people to say nice things about us after we are gone—that we were kind, generous, and honest, and that we left the world a better place. But how do we actually

Our legacy will be made of the many thousands of micro actions we take in our own small circles of influence.

- →

accomplish that? Too often, people feel that legacy is about a huge action, a large gift, or a singular memorable moment. This is true for some people, but for most of us our legacy will be made of the many thousands of micro actions we take in our own small circles of influence.

Legacy Is like Ripples in a Pond

Legacy is like ripples in a pond: You take an action, and the energy creates ripples that go beyond what you might imagine. My decision to give the unhoused person money on that hot Savannah day might have given the guy in the truck in front of me permission to do the same, just as me reading the article about the woman who always gave money gave me permission. Acts of kindness are contagious; unfortunately, so are acts of cruelty. What ripples do you want to spread?

Your legacy will reflect your personal impact. It is also the impact that, by virtue of your day-to-day choices, you can most control. You get to decide where you want to spend your time and energy. Then you move forward with the clarity that you are making an impact on your corner of the world, however large or small that corner may be.

↓

↓

↓

Ari Honarvar
San Diego, California

What goal are you working toward?
Reparative re-humanization of vulnerable and often demonized populations. I focus on refugees and asylum seekers.

What motivates you?
I was born and raised in Iran, and when I was 6 years old, women lost their right to ride a bicycle or sing in public, and music and dancing became illegal. Freedom of expression was curtailed as fundamentalists took over the government. Poetry and storytelling became my sanctuary from the horror.

What does your work look like?
I work with two nonprofit organizations. Gente Unida focuses on migrant children, and Musical Ambassadors of Peace (MAP) focuses on the healing power of music and dancing. Bringing music, dance, art, and a robust practice of savoring pleasant moments to more communities and individuals is an important part of our daily resilience diet.

How do you find and build community?
The Dancing with Refugees program is an outgrowth of MAP. Its cofounders, Cameron Powers and Kristina Sophia, utilized music's transformative power for more than two decades to build cultural bridges. Shortly after the American-led invasion of Iraq, they traveled to Baghdad and began playing and singing in the streets. The Iraqi people were seeing a different side of America. When I heard that, I knew I wanted to work with them. I recited Rumi's poetry in Farsi and English to music and

told stories about my childhood during the war to educate an audience about the beautiful side of the Middle East that's rarely featured in the news.

Who are your role models?
Robin Wall Kimmerer and bell hooks are invaluable in keeping in mind the intersectionality and interrelationality of social justice work. I'll forever remain in awe of Nasrin Sotoudeh, the Iranian attorney who has spent years in prison under horrific conditions and still defies compulsory hijab laws and continues to defend women's rights in Iran.

What keeps you going?
Participating in hundreds of dance sessions with new refugees who are struggling on so many levels has convinced me that what's good for them is good for the rest of us.

What would you want to tell your younger activist self?
Beware that even humanitarian organizations can be quite dysfunctional and cause damage with far-reaching effects. Find competent colleagues and comrades who are as committed to their own healing and the health of their relationships (including professional ones) as they are to the cause.

Do you have an intentional practice of self-care?
I practice what I teach in my Resilience Through Joy workshops and orient myself toward what's pleasing in the moment and what's right in my world; it often involves movement of some kind and being in nature. Increasing our capacity for joy also increases our capacity for suffering and dealing with trauma and the challenges of being activists. Joy is the sustainable fuel that we can rely on to pause when we need to and keep going when we need to.

We have a responsibility to be good ancestors. We are all connected, and the things we do will have impacts we never imagined.

--→

When you are intentional about the legacy you want to leave behind, you create a road map for your life. Ask yourself, "Is this action one that I want to be part of my legacy?" If yes, full speed ahead. If no, realize you've gotten off track and recalibrate to get back to doing the work that is yours to do in the way that is yours to do it. At the end of each day, you can assess and see if you moved toward or away from the legacy you wish to leave. If you've moved toward it, congratulate yourself and commit to doing the same tomorrow. If you've moved away from it, gently recognize where you went wrong and correct your course tomorrow.

BE A GOOD ANCESTOR

Layla F. Saad, author of *Me and White Supremacy*, speaks about the importance of being a good ancestor and using this as the metric for the choices she makes in life. Being a good ancestor means being a good steward of what is here that needs protecting: our families, friends, neighbors, all living creatures, and the earth. But it's also about looking beyond personal concerns to the concerns of the collective. Yes, we want to take care of those closest to us and to leave a good legacy for them, but if that is where our concern ends, we aren't actually leaving the legacy we think we are. Part of leaving a good legacy is recognizing that we are part of something much bigger than our individual selves and our individual families. We are part of the human family. We are part of life on this earth, and we honor or dishonor the responsibility that comes with being part of a collective by the actions we choose to take.

Whether or not we have biological connections to future generations, we have a responsibility to be good ancestors. We are all connected, and the things we do will have impacts we never imagined.

In our fast-paced world it can be easy to rush through our days, weeks, and months—and ultimately our lives— without taking stock of what we are doing and the impact of our actions both immediate and long-term. It can be easy to override our knowing that a certain decision may have a short-term benefit but long-term negative consequences. Holding the lens of legacy, of being a good ancestor, can keep us from selling out our long-term goal for the immediate fix.

THINK OF LEGACY AS THE PRESENT, NOT THE FUTURE

When you take the concept of legacy out of the realm of "someday in the future" and move it to "today," it becomes much more accessible. We don't get bogged down in lofty ideas of what legacy "should" be and instead can focus on what it is: the choices we make and the actions we take on a daily basis that send ripples out into the world. Imagine how thinking about each choice you make as part of your legacy would impact your daily behavior. Would you still make mistakes that needed cleaning up? Sure, mistakes are part of being human. But holding the concept of legacy as part of your regular framework will encourage you to do the hard work of trying to make things right when you've done harm rather than passing along unhealed harm.

Staying connected to legacy as part of what you are building each day keeps you present to your mission in a world full of distractions. It's your "true north" when the siren song of "shallow" is singing, calling you away from the deep work that is most likely to leave the impact you desire to make.

Nina Altschiller

Savannah, Georgia

What are you working toward?

Voting rights.

What motivates you?

I was born into a political family. My father was elected to Congress when I was 2 years old. Until I was 13, I could go onto the floor of the House of Representatives and watch the proceedings. He was a cosponsor of the Voting Rights Act and was an active participant in the floor debate. I was there when it was passed, and I was in the Rotunda when it was signed. To say that it made an impact would be a major understatement. The first time I voted, I voted for myself. I was 20 and running to be a McGovern delegate. I won and was one of a handful of new voters at the convention.

What does your work look like?

It looks like billboards and clipboards and online meetings. Lots of meetings.

How do you find and build community?

The community existed; I just joined them. In 2020, I ran the Get Out the Vote (GOTV) effort for the League of Women Voters of Coastal Georgia. The following year they asked me to be president. Since then, I've been networking, doing speaking engagements, social media, and lots of basic political glad-handing.

> Every activist is doing Sisyphean work. There's no such thing as winning or losing.

Who are your role models?
My father, first and foremost.

What keeps you going when things are hard?
My father. He's long dead but still very much in my head. I still work for his approval.

What do you want to tell your younger activist self?
Don't be so strident. You don't know it all. Don't take yourself so seriously. You have so much to learn.

What do you want to tell your future activist self?
Don't give up. There's so much more to do.

Do you have an intentional practice of self-care?
Yoga. Heart-to-heart conversations with friends. Too much wine. Every activist is doing Sisyphean work. There's no such thing as winning or losing. There's just work. It's hard and it's rewarding and it's daunting. Incremental victories followed by less incremental setbacks equal success. It pays poorly or not at all. We all wonder why we do it. But the little victories make it all worthwhile.

↓
↓
↓

Connect with Your Why and Who

Another part of leaving an intentional legacy is to deeply connect with your *why* and your *who*. Why are you doing this work? And who are you doing it for? Answering these questions will guide you when things get hard and when you struggle to motivate yourself. For me, I'm doing my activist work, in part, for my brother's children. They deserve a beautiful, safe, healthy, and welcoming world in which to live. I want my legacy to be that I did what I could to make that a reality for them.

Legacy doesn't have to be loud to be meaningful. All four of my grandparents emigrated to the United States from the Caribbean. They left family and jobs to seek a better life in a country that wasn't as welcoming to them as it could have been. My grandparents made the best of it. They sent all six of their children to college; two of their sons went to Ivy League schools, and one of their daughters became a physician. My grandparents worked at jobs below their skill and training levels because racism narrowed the opportunities available to them. I don't recall them complaining, although they probably did, just not in front of us grandkids. What I remember most is that they were tenacious and refused to stop striving for the goals of equal justice and opportunity that they undoubtedly knew they would not live to see realized. My paternal grandmother was, at 101, living in a nursing home and on a committee petitioning the mayor of New York and other officials to mandate better food in nursing homes. (The word *badass* definitely applied to Grandma Georgianna.)

My grandparents, like so many others, did what they did not only for themselves but also for those who would come after them, and we are forever grateful. My generation's debt to them can be repaid only by carrying on the work they did on our behalf. I don't have to take up their exact cause, but I respect them by working toward my own cause with the same level of persistence they showed. My grandparents set a high standard of dignity, respect, and tenacity for their children and grandchildren—and they are largely unknown outside our family, just like millions of other people who do remarkable, yet unremarked upon, things each and every day.

HARM ALSO HAS A LEGACY

On the other side of the equation are those who leave a legacy that is less admirable than that of my grandparents, a legacy of hurt and harm. The work of social justice is to repair the harm that has been done over centuries and generations, and still lives on in the legacies of environmental greed and degradation, the very present damage of slavery, and the injustice of colonialism.

Asking yourself "Who will this action help? Who will this action hurt?" is a way of taking a longer, broader view of what you are considering doing. A long view will help make it far more likely that the legacy you leave is the one you intend to leave.

BEING AT FAULT VS. TAKING RESPONSIBILITY

It is important to recognize that there is a difference between being at fault for something and taking responsibility. No one alive today in the United States is at fault for the evils of slavery as it existed in the past. But it is the responsibility of everyone alive today to recognize the evil of the seeds that have flourished as a result of slavery, and to do what they can to undo that evil and to bring equity and justice to our world.

Most of us are not directly at fault for the climate catastrophe that the world is facing, but we are all responsible for taking action to help us avoid the worst impacts of climate change. Looking through the lens of legacy, decisions become clearer and actions that flow from those decisions can be more aligned with our values.

Don Estill

Los Angeles, California

What are you working toward?

Elevating Black stories, focusing on the experiences of Black women.

What motivates you?

Tarana Burke, whom I consider one of our greatest modern-day agents of change. Burke's experiences of feeling removed from a movement that she created is one of the reasons why I created a documentary on the voices of Black women. My love, admiration, and appreciation for my mother, Wanda, who passed away in 2013, is the other.

What does your work look like?

I'm producing a one-hour documentary that is centered around Black female voices. It highlights how Black women thrive and shine in a society that often devalues their very existence. I started by having a dialogue with Black women from various ages and backgrounds. I asked, "Do you ever feel like you are not heard?" We put the responses on film and created the documentary *She Speaks*.

I'm also creating a nonprofit organization that would use the concept of guaranteed income to help working single Black mothers. The goal is to give $1,000 per month to working mothers to use how they see fit over a 12- to 18-month period and see what change it brings to their lives. I have found a young woman who would benefit greatly from having a guaranteed income. My plan is to create a study about the effects that it has on her family (two young boys) and her life. She currently is in a

> **There is nothing about my Black skin that means I do not deserve to live a life without fear or worry. I am rightfully here.**

trade school and works full time at a fast-food restaurant. She aspires to be a lawyer. I want the program to grow to create financial resources and mentorships that would help her achieve her goal.

Who are your role models?
Tarana Burke, Emil Wilbekin, Stacey Abrams, Lucy McBath, Sybrina Fulton, Malcom X, Bayard Rustin.

What keeps you going?
My ancestors and spirit guides. I have the utmost faith in what I physically cannot see but what I spiritually feel. I surround myself with good friends that I consider family. My brothers, sisters, nieces, and nephews always bring me a great deal of joy. I believe we need to tear down the system that continues to belittle and devalue Black life. There is nothing about my Black skin that means I do not deserve to live a life without fear or worry. I am rightfully here. My life should not be made small to make others feel better about themselves. I have the right to exist, and I will fight with every ounce of my being for that right.

What would you tell your activist self from 10 years ago?
You are going to see the worst in people. You will lose some so-called friends, but your passion and heartfelt love for your people will change lives, your own included. Do not give up!

↓
↓
↓

Your Past and Future Legacy

▶ **Who are the people in my family** who left a legacy that I admire?

▶ **Are there people in my family who left a legacy that I am trying to repair?** If so, who are they and what is the wrong I am trying to set right?

▶ **How can I allow myself** to take responsibility for making reparations without taking on guilt?

▶ **What is the legacy** I want to leave?

▶ **Who are the people** I want to leave this legacy for?

▶ **What would leaving a good legacy** look like for me?

▶ **Who are the people in my life** and the people I have never met whose legacies inspire me?

▶ **How can I use this inspiration** to inform the work I do in the world?

Activism and Kids

For many people, legacy is deeply connected to children, whether they're our own or those of others. The values that we pass on to the children we have, and to those we are entrusted to educate or care for, can be a huge part of our legacy.

I do not have biological children, but I take tremendous pleasure in the activist work I do with young people, and I consider those youth to be part of my legacy. When I work with, teach, and learn from children, I get to witness the cycle of legacy in action. I teach them, I learn from teaching them, they learn from me, they teach me, and around it goes. When I am gone from here, they will, I hope, take the best of what I have given them and share it with those who will be part of their own legacy.

Children are open and curious about everything. Their openness inspires me to be more open and less rigid in my beliefs. Their curiosity pushes me to look for ideas outside the ones that I come up with as solutions to challenges that I am confronting.

ASK AND LISTEN

Children also have a strong sense of fairness and justice. As adults who are caring for and educating them, we have an opportunity to guide them as they find the causes that speak to them. We can help them find their path of activism. Kids care deeply about things. Too often, we adults are too busy doing other things to listen to them and hear their concerns. When we take the time to listen and ask questions, we often find that children's understanding of issues is far more sophisticated than we give them credit for. We also often find that they want to do something to make a positive difference and simply need a little bit of help in figuring out what they want to do and the best way to do it.

In a world obsessed with self-promotion, activism encourages kids to be selfless.

Supporting kids in becoming active in a cause not only benefits whatever cause they are advocating for but also builds their sense of agency and their understanding that they are part of a community and that their actions matter. In a world obsessed with self-promotion, activism encourages kids to be selfless.

STAY OPEN AND CURIOUS

Have you ever noticed how kids are willing to try pretty much anything? They don't come to a challenge with a predetermined set of reasons why something won't work (which we as adults often do). They show up with open hearts and minds, a willingness to try something and to see what happens. They seem equipped with an instinctual belief that they *can* make a difference—until adults make them think otherwise.

We can learn a lot from kids' openness and their uncomplicated desire to fix what they see as wrong. Our job is to nurture that desire, to let children lead the way even when we think there is a better way. There may well be a better way, but allowing kids to find *their* way goes far in building their confidence down the road. Letting kids be creative and self-reliant has huge implications for their faith in themselves later. If we can view our role as one of simply making sure that what they are doing is safe, and then stepping back and being supportive, we help lay the groundwork for kids to use their voices and their talents to make the world that they are living in better.

NURTURE THE HABIT OF ACTIVISM

The habits that we develop as children tend to stay with us throughout our lives. Nurturing the habit of activism is one of the best things we can do for the children in our orbit. Raising children who care about other people, who see justice as a value worth fighting for, and who know that this is their work to do as much as anyone else's is a tremendously worthwhile legacy to leave.

If there are children in your life, have you talked with them about the things in the world that they wish were different? Do you tend to think they are "too young" for certain conversations? Of course, that can be the case, but we often underestimate kids' capacity. There are age-appropriate ways to talk about hard subjects like racism and gun violence. It has been said that if a child is old enough to experience something, they are old enough to talk about it.

Even though there are experiences that no child should have to endure—active shooter drills in school, for example— we should give children going through those experiences some agency in expressing their feelings about them. They can often tell us what they would do to change things.

Kelli Stewart

Atlanta, Georgia

What are you working toward?

Restorative justice. I do not believe that racism can or will be eradicated; however, we have a responsibility to restore those of us who have been and are injured by it.

What motivates you?

My grandmother's name is Amy Lou Faust. She was born into the racist system of sharecropping in a small town called Crawford, Georgia. She is the oldest ancestor I know and had a relationship with; she raised me. As I've learned about what it means to be Black in America, I understand how much was taken from her—dignity, opportunity, safety, security. I fight for her, myself, my family, and my community.

What does your work look like?

My activism is in sport-based youth development programming and policy for Black youth in 6th through 12th grades in the Atlanta Public Schools. We provide year-round, sports-based youth development programming for at-risk boys from low-income households, and who are underperforming in grades, attendance, or behavior. Our boys are also categorized as dysregulated, meaning they experience intense, frequent levels of trauma due to socioeconomic stressors caused by crime, poverty, and racism. The most powerful buffer for our youth growing up in these circumstances is frequent, consistent interaction with our coaches and mentors who provide empowering, challenging, positive youth development experiences.

> The most powerful buffer for our youth growing up . . . is frequent, consistent interaction with our coaches and mentors who provide empowering, challenging, positive youth development experiences.

How do you find and build community?
Sports is inherently a community-building activity. Baseball, particularly, was seen as a rite of passage for men during the era of the Negro Leagues, and when Jackie Robinson broke the color barrier it was the sport that showed us that Black and white professionals could play together.

Who are your role models?
Georgia Gilmore, Shirley Chisholm, Fred Hampton, Malcolm X, Dr. Martin Luther King Jr., and Coretta Scott King.

What keeps you going?
When things get tough, I imagine how tough things must have been for my grandmother. The fact that I'm still alive is a testament to how hard she fought. She survived, and I must do the same. When I was young, I was the brunt of many racial jokes and didn't know it; but the white kids knew. I encourage all African Americans, especially the elders in the family, to share their experiences. I know sharing and reliving trauma is tough, but it's necessary for those of us who only read about the struggle to learn and understand so we can be ready to stand, fight, and heal.

Do you have an intentional practice of self-care?
I absolutely love to sing and chill with my husband and daughters. Singing helps me release stress and live out the dreams that I never got to see through.

↓
↓
↓

GET KIDS INVOLVED

Are there children in your orbit who could tell you their areas of concern about the world? Who are those kids? Make a list. Set aside some time to brainstorm with them on ways they can make a positive difference.

What are some age-appropriate ways in which you might include children in your activist pursuits? Check out the resources section (page 171) for some child-focused organizations that are doing wonderful work in the activist realm.

Chapter Takeaways

DEEPLY CONSIDER what you want your legacy to be and how you can make that vision a reality.

Remember that your legacy is **BUILT PIECE BY PIECE.** Each day is an opportunity to build what you want.

NURTURING ACTIVISM in children will impact your legacy and set kids on the path to becoming changemakers.

⬇
⬇
⬇

→ Maintaining Momentum

Congratulations! You have worked your way through most of this book. You've looked at some limiting beliefs around what constitutes being an activist, you've identified your activist archetype, and you've narrowed down your areas of focus to one or, at most, two causes. You've also spent some time engaged in radical realism, bringing your expectations of yourself in alignment with the reality of your life. You've explored the idea of deep work versus shallow work, and you've begun to free yourself from the tyrannical thinking of big impact, competition, and comparison. You've thought deeply about the legacy you wish to leave and how to connect that to your micro activism.

That is a lot! Putting these realizations and new ways of thinking into practice in your activism will benefit you not only in the cause that you are focused on but also in your life. There is enormous satisfaction to be gained when we point ourselves in a clear direction and make a plan to get there. You've done the bulk of the work already; now let's make your plan! Before you get started, I hope you take a little bit of time to acknowledge yourself for all that you have done so far.

Making Activism Routine

The goal is that activism, in some way, tiny or large, becomes part of your daily routine, just like brushing your teeth. When activism becomes so automatic that you don't have to decide to do it, you just slot it into your life, you keep building the legacy you want to leave.

Having a regular routine of activism takes it out of the "things I have to decide to do" realm and moves it into the "things I don't think about but do regularly" realm. Building your activist efforts into your day or week frees up a lot of brain space that you can use for the work itself instead of deciding if you're going to do the work.

THE MAGIC OF COMMUNITY

As I discussed in Chapter 4, I recommend making your work a communal effort. That could mean 20 people or just 1 other person, and that other person could be your child or your best friend. We are more likely to honor commitments that we make to other people than those that we promise ourselves. (This is human nature. Why spend energy fighting it?)

Part of what we are trying to do here is to make activism so easy to do that the mere idea of not doing it seems silly. If you promised someone that you would make a weekly call to your state legislator's office, just the thought "I said

I would call" can motivate you. And when you do make the call, using a script written by someone who is part of your activist community—meaning you don't have to do all the research on your own (divide and conquer)—will save you time and energy.

MICRO ACTIONS ARE MIGHTY

The whole point of micro actions is that they are sustainable in a way that large actions often are not. Micro actions can be squeezed into small amounts of time, don't take much energy, and yet have a cumulative effect that is disproportionate to the individual effort they require.

Even if you are taking on a larger task, you can apply the same principles. For example, let's say your goal is to reach 250 voters in support of a candidate before the upcoming school board election, and your task is to write postcards. If you spend 10 to 15 minutes a day, 5 days a week, and write 5 postcards each day, in 10 weeks you will have hit your target without struggling. In a school board election, where a tiny percentage of people vote, your postcards can have a disproportionate impact.

Strategy Is as Important as Size

With micro activism, strategy is as important as size. Spending a little time on your strategy at the beginning of your planning, being realistic about your goals and what you can reasonably commit to doing, will pay off in terms of your ability to sustain your activism over the long term.

I've long been fascinated by how different societies approach planning. I learned that in Japan, it is common business practice to plan 50 years out. In the United States, a 5- or 10-year plan is more the norm. What fascinated me about the way the Japanese approached their planning was that the planners knew that, unless they were quite young, they would likely not live to see their plan come to fruition, and they were fine with that. The long-term goal had value over short-term satisfaction.

All the wonders of the world—the magnificent cathedrals of Europe, the temples of the Mayans—were built over hundreds of years. I am struck by the generosity and dedication of the architects and artisans who created something for those who would come after them. These structures, in their beauty and complexity, were their legacy.

As you make your plan, keep legacy in the forefront of your mind. Focusing on your desired legacy will make it easier to make decisions about where you will and will not spend your time. Those ancient architects left remarkable legacies, and so did the artisans and workers who worked to bring their vision to life. Every stone carver, every person who hauled the stones, and every person who placed the stones left a legacy. That most of their stories are lost to time doesn't diminish the magnitude of their accomplishments.

TAKE INCREMENTAL STEPS

Every marcher in Selma, Alabama, on Bloody Sunday—and everyone in all the days of protests and marches before—left a legacy of a bit more freedom than existed when they took up their cause. Every environmentalist who has made it their business to alert us to the dangers of climate change has helped move us toward action. In both these cases, the fact that the goal has not yet been achieved doesn't mean that the work that's been done hasn't made a difference. The millions of incremental steps that come before the tipping point are what creates the tipping point.

As you create your own plan, keep the idea of incremental steps in mind. That will help you avoid the pitfall of trying to do too much at once and burning out. Activism can easily result in burnout because there is so much to do, and emotional overload can show up when we lose focus on our goals. If, instead of looking through a broad lens, you keep your focus narrow and your goals readily attainable (micro activism anyone?), you will find that you are building your activist muscle and your capacity for taking more action should you choose to do more.

DRAW OUT YOUR HIDDEN SKILLS

Go back to the list you created in Chapter 2, the one you whittled down to your top one or two areas of focus.

Now make a list of all the things that you are really good at and like to do. Your list might include things like cooking, crafts, graphic design, driving, or even construction. The items don't have to seem like they have anything to do with activism; just make your list as comprehensive as you can.

The reason for creating this list is that there are always seemingly unrelated skills that come in handy in activism, because every single cause we're fighting for is part of life on this planet. So, if you've got construction skills, you can certainly help build homes for the unhoused or a platform for a speaker at a rally. If you've got graphic design ability, then you could help design a poster that gets put up around town in support of a candidate for public office or a cause.

If you're a good cook, you could help keep the campaign staff fed while they're putting in long days getting out the vote, or you could volunteer at a local shelter to help feed those in need. Are crafts your thing? How about volunteering at an after-school arts program that's filling the gap created by budget cuts?

Whatever your skill set, there is a way to use those skills to serve your community and to advance your cause.

Okay, you've got your list. Now think of ways that your skills could be used in service of your cause. Don't worry about who it is that you're going to offer these skills to; just make your list, and we'll get to the *who* later.

You Don't Have to Know Everything Before You Begin

Now it's time to think about your education. I'm not talking about going back to school; I'm talking about making sure that you are reasonably well informed on your area of interest. If you're interested in working on reproductive rights, are you aware of what the current laws are in your state? Do you know which organizations are working on the issue locally and statewide? What bills are currently being proposed by your state legislature around this issue? Those are examples of some of the knowledge that will be helpful to have.

You don't have to know everything before you start taking action. Think of this as the work of a school year: If you're at the beginning of the semester, you don't have to cram; you can learn as you go along. Even if you feel that you should be further along in your knowledge than you are, just keep learning. There's always more to learn, and the most important thing is to stay open to knowledge no matter when you start.

DON'T GET DISCOURAGED IF YOU HAVE TO LEARN THINGS

You can take action even if you feel there is still a lot for you to learn. Of course, you don't want to do something that requires knowledge you don't yet have, but don't let the fact that you don't know everything (as if anyone could ever know everything) keep you from both getting in the game and learning as you go along.

Make a list of some sources of education that you can tap. Search the internet about your focus area. While you're at it, search for groups doing work nearby. Look at newspapers and magazines. And don't forget to ask friends and colleagues if they have suggestions (I'm often surprised by how wide some people's range of interests and knowledge are). Do these simple steps, and you will be pointed in the direction of people, groups, and media that will help you expand your knowledge.

CONNECT TO YOUR COMMUNITY

Okay, you've identified gaps in your knowledge and ways to begin to fill those gaps. Now it's time to think about the community that you would like to work with. Even if you're a dedicated loner, associating yourself with a community that is working in your area of focus will help you. People in that community will have institutional knowledge and resources that you can use as you plan your work. For example, they will likely know who the allies are in your state legislature, who needs bringing along, and who should just be voted out of office.

Here, again, is where the internet is your friend. Search for organizations that intersect with your interests that are located in your area. Start with a broad search, taking notes about the organizations you find and adding them to a document or spreadsheet. Once you have a few options, start doing some basic research. Check out the organization's website. Based on what you see on their site, do they feel like a good fit for you and your core values? If they are local, ask around and see what you can find out. Have people you trust had experience with this organization? Have those experiences been mostly positive or mostly negative? What is their tax status? If they are a 501(c)(3) charitable organization, they are required to make their financial reports available to the public, and you can see how much of their funding goes directly to programs.

If an organization has been around for a while, it should have a network that you can both rely on and offer your skills to. Ideally, its members will also have a more finely honed sense of the dynamics at play in your community around their issue and some strategies for successfully navigating those dynamics. I want to point out that longevity isn't necessarily a good metric for how functional a group is; sometimes longevity becomes rigidity as people want to do what they've always done. New organizations can bring a lot of energy to the work. Pay attention and trust your gut.

↓

↓

↓

How to Find Organizations to Work With

▶ **Make a list of organizations** that are doing work that aligns with your goals and values.

▶ **Make a list of ways** in which you could potentially support these organizations. Make a separate list for each organization.

▶ **Decide how you will connect** with these organizations. Will you go to one of their meetings? Will you offer your services by emailing them and letting them know what you do that might be useful to them? Will you send money?

▶ **Add a due date** for each outreach effort so that it doesn't fall through the cracks.

▶ **Determine what you can realistically do,** and make note of it. For example, you might volunteer two hours a week at the library's literacy program or work a weekly shift at the food pantry.

▶ **Great! Now cut that in half.** We typically overestimate what we can do when we are excited about something. If it turns out that your initial estimate was accurate, wonderful! But in case you were a little too enthusiastic, keeping your estimate realistic won't set you up for failure.

▶ **Do you already have friends who care about this area of activism?** If so, talk with them about teaming up to enhance your efforts and to support one another, and then get to it!

You're Ready

Woohoo! You have done it. Micro activism in your area of interest is now something for which you have a plan and a set of strategies. As I said at the beginning, our small actions accumulate, both in collective impact and in momentum. All the work that you've put in—reading, thinking, and planning—will pay off in focus and persistence. You have put together a tool kit that supports your unique way of being an activist in this world.

Let yourself be inspired by the activists you've met in these pages, as well as those you have met and will continue to meet in your own life. And remember that, for someone else, you are an inspiration.

Take a few moments to celebrate what you've learned and what you've accomplished along the way. Then find a mirror, look at yourself, and recognize that an activist looks exactly like you.

Chapter Takeaways

Make **ACTIVISM ROUTINE** and put your focus less on the size of the action and more on the habit of action.

FIND YOUR COMMUNITY. Working alongside people who care about what you care about makes all the difference.

STAY CONNECTED TO THE LEGACY you want to leave. Decision-making becomes easier when you ask yourself, Will this bring me closer to the legacy I wish to leave?

STAY OPEN TO LEARNING.

Remember that **MILLIONS OF SMALL ACTIONS** equal huge change: "Add your light to the sum of light."

↓
↓
↓

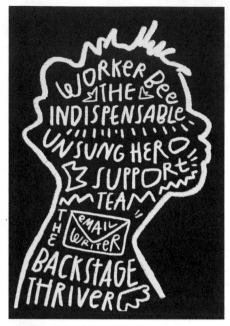

THE INDISPENSABLE: You are one of the many people working in the background to make change.

THE PRODUCER: You create the schedule and make sure that nothing falls through the cracks.

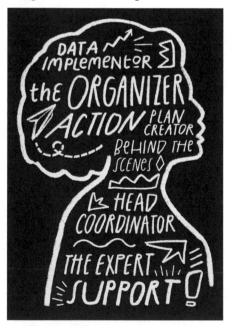

THE ORGANIZER: You keep things on schedule and address the various assignments.

THE HEADLINER: You are the face of the movement, the person who inspires those who seek the same change you do.

ACTIVIST ARCHETYPE QUIZ

Pick the answer in the following scenarios that best describes what you would do. Circle or write down your answers to these seven questions. Note that you'll likely be a combination of types. One may be dominant, or you may land equally in two archetypes. Use this quiz to help guide you as you plan for how to make micro activism part of your life.

QUESTION 1

A friend is having a fundraising event for a cause you believe in and are knowledgeable about. The day before the event, the main speaker comes down with laryngitis and your friend asks you to fill in. You:

A. Say yes as you fondly recall your days as captain of your school's debate team.

B. Tell your friend that if she absolutely can't find anyone else, you will do it; you immediately start to sweat.

C. Give your friend the names of four other people who would be better, including your 6-year-old nephew.

D. Graciously tell your friend that you would rather sit home with a sharp object in your eye.

A. Headliner **B.** Organizer **C.** Producer **D.** Indispensable

QUESTION 2

"Diversity Day" is coming to your kids' school, and you are determined to help out. You decide to:

A. Talk one-on-one with kids struggling with their identities.

B. Bake the gluten-, nut-, and sugar-free cookies.

C. Facilitate the group question-and-answer session with 50 kids.

D. Direct the puppet show that teaches the lessons of the diversity curriculum.

A. Organizer **B.** Indispensable **C.** Producer **D.** Headliner

QUESTION 3

You turn on the news and learn that people are being denied entry to the United States based on their country of origin. You immediately:

A. Send money to the American Civil Liberties Union (ACLU) and other groups taking action to stop this practice. Then you start strategizing other actions to take.

B. Write a letter to the editor of your local paper about how this country should be a refuge for people fleeing violence and tyranny.

C. Tap the most powerful connections you have and begin organizing a protest march on Washington, D.C.

D. Call and email your elected representatives to register your opposition to this practice.

A. Producer B. Indispensable C. Headliner D. Organizer

QUESTION 4

You are on the subway and see Immigration and Customs Enforcement (ICE) officers asking Brown people for proof that they are in the United States legally. You:

A. Start filming the officers on your phone and livestream it to social media.

B. Calmly engage the officers in conversation in hopes of distracting them so that undocumented people can get off at the next stop.

C. Stand up and, using your "outside" voice, tell everyone in the subway car that they are not legally required to speak with the officers and that the officers do not have the right to search them or their property without a properly executed warrant.

D. Quietly move to the next car and warn passengers that ICE is on the train.

A. Organizer B. Producer C. Headliner D. Indispensable

↓
↓
↓

QUESTION 5

As far as activism goes, your favorite thing to do is:

A. Attend a protest march. You want your voice heard, and you love the communal energy.

B. Write a letter to the editor or call and email your elected officials.

C. Start a movement!

D. Organize a protest. You're still bitter that you missed the anti–Vietnam War movement and Woodstock.

A. Producer **B.** Indispensable **C.** Organizer **D.** Headliner

QUESTION 6

You go online and see that an influencer in your area of activist interest has put her foot in her mouth in a big way. That's okay; we all make mistakes. But she's not owning it and is, instead, claiming that those calling her out are being unfair. You feel that she was wrong in what she said, so you:

A. Quietly watch and see what others are saying but don't add your opinion to the mix.

B. Direct message her and initiate a private conversation.

C. Directly and publicly engage with her in an effort to move the conversation to a broader one on the difficulties of social justice work and how we all need to be aware of our unconscious biases.

D. Start a frank discussion on the responsibility that influencers hold, and tag her.

A. Indispensable B. Producer C. Headliner D. Organizer

↓
↓
↓

QUESTION 7

You are watching the news and see 16-year-old Greta Thunberg addressing Congress about climate change. You find her impressive, and you think:

A. Her work is inspiring to me; I bet there's a way to replicate it on a much smaller scale.

B. This is the way to do things. I will work to get noticed on a huge stage so that I can make the difference I want to make.

C. Yikes! She is incredible, but the mere thought of addressing Congress makes me break out in hives. I'm happy stuffing envelopes in the back office.

D. Wow, this kid is amazing! I don't have what it takes to do what she is doing, but I am absolutely willing to take up the task.

A. Headliner B. Producer C. Indispensable D. Organizer

Now that you know your activist archetype, learn more about what kind of activist you are on pages 24–33.

GROUP GUIDE

How to Create an Activist Group

While the bulk of this book is directed toward solo acts of micro activism, the principles can work for groups of people who share a common goal. Use this guide to help structure your group to make the best use of the talents of each member. I suggest that all group members read *Micro Activism* so that you are speaking a shared language about how micro activism works as you leverage its strength in a group setting. There is much healing work to be done in this world. Doing it in community brings more joy and hope to the work. It will give you people to turn to in times of frustration, heartbreak, and anger, as well as in times of joy. Doing activist work in collaboration with others strengthens not only your personal activism but also your community. Thank you for all that you do.

Determine how your group will be structured.
One of the most important things that you can do is to determine how your group will be structured. Is there a person who is the final decision-maker, or will every significant decision require the group to find consensus? How will the meetings be structured? Will one person be the leader of all meetings, or will that job rotate so that everyone takes on a leadership role at some point? I prefer that the job of leading meetings rotates. Even the quietest person has thoughts and ideas about how to address the challenges that inspired this group to come into existence. Creating an environment where everyone gets to take a leadership role can allow for a creativity that doesn't exist when it's always the same person leading. (For more on creating this kind of group process I recommend the book *The Circle Way* by Christina Baldwin and Ann Linnea.) How you structure your group will also help establish how you are going to address conflict when it inevitably arises (more on this later).

Set the ground rules. Once you've got your basic structure sorted out, make ground rules for the group. Set your parameters on basic things like the length, frequency, and location of meetings. Doing this at the outset allows people to understand what they are committing to and reduces the friction that comes from unclear expectations. If you don't have a set location for your meetings, you may want to plot out meeting location arrangements for at least a few meetings ahead of time. Depending on the size of your group, you might want to explore free (or very inexpensive) space at a local school or community center. If there is an associated cost for the space, decide how the group will cover that. Remember that what may be a small cost for one person may not be a small cost for another. Be aware of making assumptions about who can afford what.

Zero in on your group's focus. When people form or join a group it's easy to think that everyone interested in the cause is on the same page. But people have different areas of focus and differing opinions even under the larger umbrella of the activist cause. Determine what the specific focus of your group will be. It is especially important in small groups to narrow your area of work so that what you do has the greatest impact possible. When I say impact here, I'm not talking about the size of the action. I'm talking about making sure that you are using your time and energy as effectively as possible. Of course, you want to be efficient, but this is even more important when there are only a few people doing the work. You don't want to burn out anyone, including yourself.

Keep your focus narrow. Remember to apply the Noah's ark rule (page 52) to group projects. Use the rule to keep your group's focus narrowed. For example, your sole focus might be

↓

↓

↓

getting five unhoused veterans into five tiny homes that are built to accommodate the special needs they have. Although you want to solve the whole problem of unhoused vets in your area eventually, right now your focus is on housing just five people to start. As you build relationships, credibility, and power, you can expand your mission, but start with a goal that feels possible within the parameters of your group.

Discover everyone's activist archetype. Once you've determined your area of focus, it is a good time to find out what the different members' activist archetypes are (page 24) so that you can see which roles are filled and where you might need someone with a particular archetype. You don't need to have someone from each archetype in your group, but if you don't have one archetype then you will need to figure out who can step into a certain role that may be a bit outside their comfort zone. Or, as a group you can fill some of the roles that you're missing. For example, the group as a whole may be able to fill the role of the Producer by taking on various tasks of that archetype so that the larger picture is clear at all times. If you are still missing people who can do various jobs, it's a good time to look for people you might invite to join your group who have the skill sets and temperament to fill the gaps. Part of micro activism is being willing to stretch yourself a bit so that you keep growing (as individuals and as a group) in your capacity to make the change that you are seeking.

Make a comprehensive list. Ask each member of the group to participate in making a comprehensive list of all the things that you can think of that will need to be done to get your project from start to finish. Every single tiny action that you can think of should go on this list. This is one of the places where groups shine. One person can't possibly think of all the things that will need to be done, but a group of people will be more likely to identify all the critical aspects (and some bonus ideas) for actions you can take. Having this list will be a huge help as you work on your overall plan. While you'll want to start this list early, be sure to keep adding to it as different needs present themselves.

Divide up the tasks. Now that you have a list of tasks, divide them up by archetype so that you're matching people with their strongest skills. This is also an opportunity for people to do a bit of stretching outside their comfort zone. You want to pay attention though so that no one is taking on the lion's share of the work. It doesn't have to be evenly divided but if you notice that one person has a lot on their plate, that's the time to invite other group members to take on some of the tasks that need filling. Leverage the group. Within the context of your overall goal, what needs to get done? What resources will you need? Who knows someone who could help with providing those resources? Does someone have a connection to City Hall, or to a contractor with a soft spot for your cause, or to a friend who is a fundraiser? Most of us know more people in positions that could be helpful than we are aware of. Build a database of potential allies.

Keep notes. It is very important to keep good notes on the things that you are doing, the people you're meeting, the ideas that you have, all of it. If it pertains to your overarching goal, having it written down somewhere that everyone can access makes all the difference, not only as you do your work, but also as a record for people coming on later or taking over the work as your original team moves into different roles. Think of it as your team's operating manual. This is the record that tracks your progress as your team's mission evolves and grows.

↓

↓

↓

Map your plan. At this point you should have a good sense of who can fulfill which roles. Excellent! It's time to move on to mapping out your larger plan. Let's say your goal is to get five unhoused veterans in your community into tiny homes specifically adapted for them. What are some of the large tasks that you need to accomplish? By when? Do you have the answers you need to move forward? These might include things like researching available locations for tiny homes in your community, or understanding the costs of building and sustaining a tiny home relative to the minimum wage where you live or to veteran's benefits. What is the general relationship between the unhoused and the housed community? What are the demographics of the unhoused veterans in your community, including age and disability status? Who are the decision-makers that you will need to build relationships with? How can you build community support? Should the tiny homes be in one area or located in different areas? When do you need the answers to these questions to stay on track with your overall plan? Throughout this process everyone in the group should be making lists of all the things that they think of relating to this project so that they can be put into the larger picture you're developing.

Do some research. We tend to want to start fresh, but do not reinvent the wheel. Research what other communities have successfully done to address this problem. Then have someone reach out to those communities for a conversation that can enhance your group's understanding of the challenges and opportunities that exist. As you're doing your research, don't neglect to ask those who have been doing this work for a while about any mistakes they made or obstacles they ran into, and take notes. This knowledge can help you create a plan to navigate likely pitfalls. Better to learn from someone else's misstep than to make it yourself.

Distribute the work. Divide and conquer. Take advantage of the numbers that you have, even if it's just you and a friend, to make the workload more manageable. And remember, small actions. Avoid spreading yourself too thin, especially in the first flush of excitement as you embark on your project.

Address conflict as it arises. In groups, you can experience conflicting ideas, opinions, and ways of working. Most of us are conflict averse, but conflict is a normal part of the process and when we navigate it well it can help us make our activist plan better. Putting methods in place for addressing conflict when it arises will remove a big obstacle. Understand that conflict is likely to happen (even though not desired). When conflict is unexpected it can trigger a whole other set of tricky emotions. But if you know that it is an inevitable part of working in groups, you won't panic when it arises. Your plan can be as simple as listening to each person without interruption or feedback, and then sleeping on it, or your plan can be more in depth. You get to make the rules. Once you've made the rules, you need to follow them so that everyone is on the same page. If the rules need revision, then have that conversation separately from the conversation about the issue that sparked the conflict. Very importantly, keep the discussion on topic. Once you're in a conflict there is a tendency to bring up other upsets you've experienced. Keep the discussion focused on the issue at hand. This will prevent things from devolving into a messy, unfocused, unproductive conversation. Most of all, remember that everyone is operating from what they genuinely believe to be the best way forward. Extending grace to one another keeps a disagreement over policy or methods from becoming personal.

Have regular check-ins. Be sure that you're checking in regularly with each individual member of the group about how their specific efforts are going, where they are having successes, and where they are coming up against obstacles. It can be easy to focus on the more vocal members in the group and to lose track of the quieter members. Make sure that there is a structure in place for regularly hearing from everyone.

Revisit your plan. Schedule periodic meetings where you revisit the goals, strategies, and tactics that you have been using to guide your work. Sometimes we can get so involved in the work that we forget to take a step back and evaluate how what we're doing is actually going. A quarterly review is a good idea so that you're sure you're keeping the main point front and center.

Celebrate your wins. Big and small, celebrate what your team is accomplishing. You found a contractor who's willing to donate some work hours to your goal? Celebrate! The local stationery store will do your printing at a deeply discounted rate? Celebrate. You had a conversation with some of the vets you hope to have homes built for and got their buy in? Celebrate. The challenges and setbacks will be many—celebrate the wins. Remember that what we are *for* is stronger, and ultimately more motivating and sustainable, than what we're against. Staying connected to what your group is for is key to doing this work long-term.

Be social outside the work. I strongly recommend scheduling time for the group to get together and be social. A lunch or dinner or some activity that you can all share. Having cohesion beyond the activist work you are doing will make your group stronger and more fun. We are all multi-faceted people; recognizing and engaging across the richness of who we are, matters.

RESOURCES

BOOKS

Against Civility: The Hidden Racism in Our Obsession with Civility by Alex Zamalin

An Abolitionist's Handbook: 12 Steps to Changing Yourself and the World by Patrisse Cullors

Are Prisons Obsolete? by Angela Y. Davis

Bad Feminist: Essays by Roxane Gay

Caste: The Origins of Our Discontents by Isabel Wilkerson

James Baldwin: Collected Essays by James Baldwin

Do the Work!: An Antiracist Activity Book by W. Kamau Bell and Kate Schatz

Eloquent Rage: A Black Feminist Discovers Her Superpower by Brittney Cooper

Emergent Strategy: Shaping Change, Changing Worlds by adrienne maree brown

Feminism for the 99%: A Manifesto by Cinzia Arruzza, Tithi Bhattacharya, and Nancy Fraser

Good and Mad: The Revolutionary Power of Women's Anger by Rebecca Traister

How to Be an Antiracist by Ibram X. Kendi

How to Start a Revolution: Young People and the Future of American Politics by Lauren Duca

Joyous Resilience: A Path to Individual Healing and Collective Thriving in an Inequitable World by Anjuli Sherin

Killing Rage: Ending Racism by bell hooks

Living a Feminist Life by Sara Ahmed

Long Walk to Freedom by Nelson Mandela

Me and White Supremacy: Combat Racism, Change the World, and Become a Good Ancestor by Layla F. Saad

Mutual Aid: Building Solidarity During This Crisis (and the Next) by Dean Spade

↓

↓

↓

My Grandmother's Hands: Racialized Trauma and the Pathway to Mending Our Hearts and Bodies by Resmaa Menakem

Rage Becomes Her: The Power of Women's Anger by Soraya Chemaly

Shrill: Notes from a Loud Woman by Lindy West

Stamped from the Beginning: The Definitive History of Racist Ideas in America by Ibram X. Kendi

The Body Keeps the Score: Brain, Mind, and Body in the Healing of Trauma by Bessel van der Kolk

The Inner Work of Racial Justice: Healing Ourselves and Transforming Our Communities Through Mindfulness by Rhonda V. Magee

The Next American Revolution: Sustainable Activism for the Twenty-First Century by Grace Lee Boggs with Scott Kurashige

The Purpose of Power: How We Come Together When We Fall Apart by Alicia Garza

The Witches Are Coming by Lindy West

This Bridge Called My Back: Writings by Radical Women of Color by Cherríe Moraga and Gloria Anzaldúa, eds.

Trauma Stewardship: An Everyday Guide to Caring for Self While Caring for Others by Laura van Dernoot Lipsky with Connie Burk

Turn This World Inside Out: The Emergence of Nurturance Culture by Nora Samaran

Utopia for Realists: How We Can Build the Ideal World by Rutger Bregman

We Were Eight Years in Power: An American Tragedy by Ta-Nehisi Coates

Your Silence Will Not Protect You by Audre Lorde

Digital Resources

5 CALLS
https://5calls.org
Select the issues you care about most, and receive a list of calls to make to elected officials. Names, phone numbers, background information, and researched scripts are provided.

ANTIRACISM DAILY
https://the-ard.com
This site provides a daily topic and tangible ways to take action on various social justice causes. Podcasts and courses are also available.

THE BAIL PROJECT
https://bailproject.org
Members of this project are working to combat racial and economic disparities in the U.S. bail system.

BLACK LIVES MATTER
https://blacklivesmatter.com
The mission of BLM is to eradicate white supremacy and build local power to intervene in violence inflicted on Black communities.

BLACK VOTERS MATTER
https://blackvotersmatter
fund.org
The goal of this nonprofit organization is to increase voting in Black communities as a form of power and self-determination.

THE BORGEN PROJECT
https://borgenproject.org
This nonprofit organization works toward ending global poverty and hunger.

CHARITY NAVIGATOR
https://charitynavigator.org
This assessment organization allows the public to see how nonprofit organizations spend the money they raise.

COLOR OF CHANGE
https://colorofchange.org
The nation's largest online racial justice organization helps people respond effectively to injustice by designing campaigns to end practices that unfairly hold Black people back.

DAILY KOS
https://dailykos.com
This online journal—with the tagline "News You Can Do Something About"—focuses on national news and current social justice issues.

EMILYS LIST
https://emilyslist.org
Early Money Is Like Yeast (EMILY); it makes the dough rise. EMILYs List raises funds for progressive pro-choice women running for office.

FAIR FIGHT ACTION
https://fairfight.com
Political leader Stacey Abrams founded this organization to protect the vote.

INDIVISIBLE
https://indivisible.org
This grassroots movement includes thousands of local groups with a mission to elect progressive leaders and rebuild our democracy.

MOVEON
https://moveon.org
The joint website of MoveOn.org Civic Action and MoveOn.org Political Action is dedicated to helping people mobilize to create an inclusive and progressive future.

MY CIVIC WORKOUT
https://mycivicworkout.com
Subscribers can receive 5-, 10-, and 30-minute actions to help make activism a habit.

POSTCARDS TO VOTERS
https://postcardstovoters.org
You can use this site to create friendly, handwritten reminders to target voters in key elections across the United States.

PROJECT ID
https://projectid.org
This nonprofit organization helps Americans who don't have government-issued identification to obtain photo IDs so they can vote, get a job, open a bank account, secure housing, or get medical care.

RAICES (The Refugee and Immigrant Center for Education and Legal Services)
https://raicestexas.org
The mission of this nonprofit organization is "to defend the rights of immigrants and refugees, empower individuals, families, and communities, and advocate for liberty and justice."

RESISTBOT
https://resist.bot
Use this bot to turn your texts into messages that get sent to your elected representatives. It takes about 2 minutes, and you're done. Genius!

RUN FOR SOMETHING
https://runforsomething.net
This nationwide organization supports young progressive candidates who want to run for state and local office.

SANDY HOOK PROMISE
https://sandyhookpromise.org
With proven programs to help students in grades K–12 prevent school violence, shootings, and other harmful acts, Sandy Hook Promise empowers students to be active agents in the work for safe schools.

PODCASTS

SISTER DISTRICT PROJECT
https://sisterdistrict.com
This grassroots organization is dedicated to winning power in strategic state legislatures across the nation so that fair (non-gerrymandered) districts can be drawn.

THE CLIMATE INITIATIVE
https://theclimateinitiative.org
This organization provides youth with education and engagement tools to guide them as they advocate for awareness of and potential solutions to climate issues locally and globally.

WHITE SUPREMACY CULTURE
https://whitesupremacy culture.info
Run by the author Tema Okun, this site explores some elements of white supremacy culture that impact all of us.

WOODLANDS CONSERVANCY
https://woodlands conservancy.org
This local organization is dedicated to protecting what remains of Louisiana's environmentally critical forested wetlands (80 percent of which have been lost).

YES! MEDIA
https://yesmagazine.org
This nonprofit, reader-supported online and print magazine features articles on social justice, the environment, health and happiness, the economy, and democracy.

For the Wild: An Anthology of the Anthropocene

Good Ancestor Podcast: Interviews with Change-Makers and Culture-Shapers

Intersectionality Matters!, presented by the African American Policy Forum and Kimberlé Crenshaw

Irresistible: Collective Healing & Social Change

On Being with Krista Tippett

Pod Save America: A No-Bullshit Conversation About Politics

Speaking of Race, presented by the University of Alabama

Stay Tuned with Preet, presented by former U.S. Attorney Preet Bharara

Stepping into Truth: Conversations on Social Justice and How We Get Free, presented by Omkari Williams

ACKNOWLEDGMENTS

Whenever I have read the acknowledgments in a book, I'm always struck by how a work that has the name of one person, or perhaps two, on it is in fact not possible without the support of many others. I'm deeply grateful to have experienced this for myself in the writing of this book.

I am truly blessed to have remarkable people in my life who not only support me but also by the way they live their lives inspire me to keep reaching for the highest good that I'm capable of. Layla Saad, Melanie Dewberry, Elizabeth Frankel-Rivera, Runa Bird, and Coco Guthrie-Papy, I am so grateful to be on this journey with each of you. Thank you to Lisa Brown and Carol Weeg for keeping me tethered when spinning out seemed like a viable option.

To the amazing team at Storey, especially Alee Moncy and Maddy Jackson who helped guide me through this remarkable adventure, I am so grateful. And my editor, Liz Bevilacqua, thank you. This book only exists because you saw what was possible. To my agent, Katherine Latshaw, thank you for your belief in me and this project and for your passionate advocacy on my behalf.

To all the activists I've interviewed over the years, thank you for doing your work with such dedication, heart, and persistence.

And to every micro activist out there, old and new, thank you for what you are doing to bring healing to our world. I know that with each of us doing our part we will create the beautiful, just world we and those who come after us deserve to live in.